ISBN 978-1-4477-7169-2

enemiesofreason.co.uk
warmcherryade.wordpress.com
farewellprozac.blogspot.com
newstatesman.com/blogs/steven-baxter

Musings of a Monkey

By Steven Baxter

Intro

This is a collection of blogposts, largely on the Enemies of Reason[1] blog but also at Farewell Prozac[2] and other places, including the little-known and largely forgotten Warm Cherryade[3] blog. There's new stuff as well, including a version of a talk I gave to Bristol Skeptics in the Pub in February 2011, and enough footnotes to try and tie everything together and put stuff into context, I hope.

I started blogging in October 2007, and haven't stopped since, apart from the odd holiday and the odd bit of 'having a life', or whatever it's called nowadays. Once I started, I couldn't stop; it was a bit like an addiction. I think that's because, at last, I'd finally found a way of writing that really suited me. I'd always enjoyed writing, but I couldn't get my head around the planning required for narrative arcs, or anything like that; I'm not tremendously good at dialogue, and I don't do very well at characterisation either. In short, I'm a terrible fiction writer. But I've always had itchy typing fingers and have always enjoyed writing – mainly shorter articles and, in the

---

[1] enemiesofreason.co.uk

[2] farewellprozac.blogspot.com

[3] warmcherryade.wordpress.com/

case of blogging, little posts about whatever it was that pours into my brain at any one time.

Someone once described blogging as 'writing about the things I can't bear not to', and I think that's a perfect description. You blog not to a deadline or to an editor, but to that nagging voice in your head that tells you to write, because that's how you feel best at communicating. I fell in love with blogging very early on, because of that freedom, because of the ability to say whatever it was that was in my head at any time, because I could get my thoughts out there, and because of the way it challenged me as a writer to try and improve, and learn, and get better at expressing myself.

Most of my early blogposts were about tabloid rubbish and what I saw as bad journalism. I have been a journalist at some of the country's most dull regional newspapers and have never hit the heights of working 'for a national', but then again I never really wanted to[4]. I was always happy farting out the same old bits and bobs for whatever fools had taken me on at the time. But I did despair a little when I saw the kind of rubbish that some tabloids would come out with, particularly on subjects like immigration; as a so-called journalist, even not a very good one, there was a part of me that felt it was letting the side down to pander to stereotypes and to twist stories to fit an agenda.

---

[4] I have had the warm pleasure and delight of working such prestigious newspapers as the Staines Guardian, the Andover Advertiser and the Surrey Comet. Never let it be said I don't know what I'm talking about. Yes, the giddy heights. I know.

A lot of my early posts consisted of looks at tabloid tales.

I wanted to get away from the 'fisking' side of blogging for this collection of posts. There are a few reasons for this, but I didn't want to quote too many bits of other people's material, or reproduce front pages etc, largely due to any problems about copyright that might dredge up; and I didn't want anyone to go combing through this book looking for things to get shirty about. So I have deliberately left that side of it to one side. I may go back and do the 'Daily Mail scum' book at some point, but that's not for now. Don't worry, though. There are bits in there. You'll see glimpses of the rage at the mainstream media. I've tried to put a bit of that in there, but not overwhelm you with it. I hope I've got the balance kind of right, though you might think I haven't, but even if you think I haven't, I hope you can understand why I've done it the way I've done it.

As well as all that, there are some new pieces that I'll flag up along the way. We'll have tremendous fun and we'll all enjoy ourselves. Won't we? Yes. Yes, we will. I suppose I should talk about the whole blogging thing first though, and how I got to be a blogger in the first place.

Initially I blogged under the allonym Anton Vowl, the name of a character in Georges Perec's book A Void[5], and for a long time that allowed me the freedom to hide away

---

[5] Gilbert Adair's amazing translation into English of the e-less novel changes the French 'Voyl' in La Disparition into Vowl. So it was Vowl that I used.

a bit. I think there are plenty of entirely understandable reasons for wanting to write under an assumed name: someone is always bound to think of you as a coward for doing so, but they may well be a knave. It's not brave to write under a photo byline and craven to write an 'anonymous' blog; it's just two different ways of doing the same thing. Not all of us are comfortable with having the first Google search that comes up under our name being our blog, particularly if we want to say some spicy things and we know that any potential employer, acquaintance or whatever can read everything we've ever written immediately. But I write more about this in the chapter called 'Killing Anton'.

At the time of writing this, I am continuing to write the Enemies of Reason blog while doing a regular media blog for the New Statesman's website. So in a sense I have become one of those faces with a photo byline, opining about stuff, and ceased to be the blogger, the character, the web persona that I used to be. Well yes, and no: I'm still very much the same soft, podgy collection of bits of bone and organs that I always was, and I don't think the way I write has changed significantly (though your mileage may vary); but there it is – in a slight sense I have been absorbed into the mainstream, in whatever mainstream way you think that writing a column for a publication like New Statesman is the mainstream. I've also done a couple of pieces for the Guardian's Comment is Free section. I don't think this has changed me or what I write, though doubtless there's someone somewhere who harks back to the glory days before it all went downhill – and that's perfectly fine, of course[6].

There was a time, as well, when I'd be pretty sweary, too. It's a crude stereotype to imagine that's a childish act, a cursing for the sake of cursing, a lack of vocabulary, an infantile way of ejaculating all over the page. No. I enjoyed it. It released a little of the anger I felt when I read certain bad bits of journalism, and allowed me the freedom to express that anger in a way that was honest. I don't swear as much as I used to; but then I don't write about the Daily Mail as much as I used to – perhaps both are a good thing, perhaps not.

I think you reach a stage when you're doing 'a media blog' when you feel like you've probably tilted at enough windmills or, as my fellow blogger Five Chinese Crackers[7] put it, shown enough times that the Emperor's got his winky out; and you have to start thinking about broadening your focus a bit. I think that's quite healthy, and if I hadn't done that, then I think I wouldn't have been able to carry on with the blog. There's only so many

---

[6] The funny thing is, when looking back over the early days of the blog, a lot of it makes me annoyed now, and I wince a bit. Which isn't to say I disown it, because I don't; but if I were writing it now (I can't, because it's about stuff that is 'then', but let's just suppose) I think I'd be a bit more measured, a bit less angry, a bit less scattergun. But that was just how it felt back then, so that was how it came out. I was learning as I was going along.

[7] www.fivechinesecrackers.com

times you can point the same things out without going out of your mind, regardless of how important a thing it might be to do; I think you run the risk of becoming burnt out if you do it too often.

Well, that's one way of putting it, I suppose, but there are other things as well, other factors that have meant I've always strayed off the path of being simply a 'media blogger', for good or ill. And one of those things is because I have itchy typing fingers and they long to write things that are silly and daft, as well as things that are earnest and sensible. That's just the way it is, I'm afraid. Since the first time I managed to put pen to paper I've wanted to be silly, rather than sensible, no matter how hard I've tried, and it just leaks out, whether I want it to or not. So every now and then I let loose a bit of fun, a parody or a spoof or something along those lines, and it makes me smile, and then I get on with the business of being serious somewhere else. But the silliness is very much part of Enemies of Reason, or all of the blogs, I suppose; without it, I'd just be a rather sour-faced old sadsack hammering away in the spare bedroom about the things that annoy me. And that would never do. That just wouldn't do, at all.

So what is blogging, then? Is it some kind of citizen journalism by another name, or is it just blowing off steam? Is it meaningful or it is just ephemera, stuff to be read and then discarded because no-one would ever consider it worthy of consigning to ink on a page? I think it's all of this and none of this. It depends on what you want your blogging to be, I suppose. You can be serious, you can be silly, you can be anything you want to be; you can maintain a serious thread through the whole business or you can write whatever you want, when a thought settles in your head like a snowflake. And that's the attraction, for me. Finally, after years of trying to write but failing to get a grasp of what I was meant to be doing, there was a way of writing that suited the episodic, stuttering way in which my brain works – one daft thought at a time, done, forgotten about, linked to other thoughts, but written about and then tossed aside, a bit. And I rather liked it. I think that's why other bloggers like it. The medium is just a way of getting across what you want to get across at a particular moment, which may be something profound or something profoundly silly.

At least, that's what it is for me, and that's the whole point: I don't think I can tell you what blogging is at all, other than what it is for me, because everyone who blogs does it in a slightly different way. There are protocols and there is etiquette and all of that; but no-one can tell you the rules of blogging, and that's very much as it should be. If it all became formalised, it would start to be a little tiresome, I think. So here it is: it's a diary that other people can read. It's a collection of thoughts. It's poetry that doesn't scan. It's political pamphleteering for the electronic age. It's mindfarts. It's all of that and none of that. Blogging is whatever you want it to be, and everything you don't want it to be. Which I rather like.

In terms of ordering the content for this collection, I tried to sort it out into various different categories – media blogging here, whiny self-pity there, attempts at humour over there – but I found that things didn't really split up in any handy way. So, much like reading a blog, you'll jump from one subject to another quite rapidly and jarringly through the entries. It's not really in any order other than how the bits ended up fitting together. I suppose that keeps the feel of a blog, even though it's on paper, which is no bad thing, really. I've separated off the bits about depression as I think it makes sense to put them all in one place, though. They're also the only posts here where I've kept the dateline in, as well, as it seems to make sense to have them pinned down to a particular point in time.

I'd kind of finished the book when the whole News of the World phonehacking business exploded everywhere, and I thought: "Bugger. I can't really not write about that, can I?" so I've done a hastily-cobbled-together chapter about that, at the end. It wouldn't really make any sense not to write about it, now that I've got the opportunity to do so. So there are just some random thoughts while the issue is still very much in chaos, and most of the things will be out of date by the time I consign them to the page… but then that is the nature of these things.

Enemies of Reason – miscellaneous meanderings

A-Z of internet commenting[8]

August 7, 2008

ALCOHOL - benign, harmless substance when consumed by anyone over 45 which is also toxic and dangerous drug when administered to YOUNG PEOPLE or FERAL YOUTH. Should be taxed when drunk by YOUNG PEOPLE but not by others, who are of course responsible and never do anything wrong.

---

[8] This was kind of a breakthrough post for me as it was cross-posted to the Liberal Conspiracy website, and I got a lot more readers because of it. I had wanted for some time to write something about how the denizens of BBC Have Your Say and various newspaper websites saw the world, so thought a list might be a good way of doing it.

AND GUESS WHO'S PAYING?!??!! - useful catch-all phrase to describe anything in which the government/state is involved. Should be used at the end of any post as punctuation or a final flourish to a well-argued and wittily brilliant excoriation of NULAB's injustices and crimes.

ARRESTED - means someone did it.

ASYLUM SEEKER - Nasty economic migrant who fools PC BRIGADE with sob story about beatings, torture, family raped and murdered etc in order to be PARASITE and live life on benefits. And guess who's paying?!?!?!

BBC, THE - Pinko commie bastard scumbags who love liberals and want our children to be gay. Bonus points for saying "I BET YOU WON'T PUBLISH THIS, COMMUNIST BBC!" whenever you submit anything to the HYS messageboard.

BINGE BRITAIN - the sudden liking for alcohol which has happened since 1997. No-one underage ever drank anything before then, but now all of a sudden everyone is drinking, from the age of four upwards, then having a fight afterwards. Anticipated by Hogarth in his famous "Gin Lane under NuLab".

BIRCH, THE - magical item which restores civic pride and makes all children into better people, simply by thrashing them with it.

BLAIR, CHERIE - bonus points for criticising haircut/size of mouth.

BLAIR, TONY - once-admired leader who embraced PC BRIGADE and LIBERAL FASCISM. Bonus points for use of 'Bliar'.

BRITISH NATIONAL PARTY - much-admired intelligent band of decent men and women who would be the best thing to happen to our country. I KNOW WHERE I'M VOTING NEXT TIME AND IT'S NOT FOR JOCK MCBOTTLER, HE'S SOLD OUR COUNTRY DOWN THE RIVER!

BROKEN BRITAIN - propensity towards violence and lawlessness never seen in country until Tony Blair was elected. Don't believe the CRIME STATISTICS!

BROWN, GORDON - please don't use his correct name. Acceptable names are Jock McBottler, Gordie McHaggis, Tartan McBroon, Jimmy McIrnBru, etc. Must be blamed for everything in the world, eg man attacked by hedgehog in New Zealand[9].

BUSH, GEORGE W - wise and noble leader of the free world. He's the only one who can see the truth!

CAMERON, DAVID - the saviour of the world. Will cure cancer with a single touch. A bit left-wing for our tastes obviously, but we'll cut him some slack until he gets

---

[9] Seriously, someone blamed Gordon Brown for a hedgehog being attacked in New Zealand. ericthefishking.blogspot.com/2008/04/cllr-chris-cooke-cocks-up-completely.html

into power and refuses to bring back the birch.

CANNABIS - a drug that kills anyone who takes it straight away.

CLARKSON, JEREMY - wittily hilarious man-of-people who sees through PC BRIGADE and all that nonsense. Classical views on GREEN ISSUES to be agreed with include deriding any environmentalist as a 'lunatic'.

CONSERVATIVE PARTY - will solve all the nation's problems when they get into power.

CRIME STATISTICS - keep going down, but I don't believe that because some bloke in the pub told me that kids are getting let off with a caution for rape and murder nowadays, so there.

CRIMINALS - Get let off with a 'mind how you go' by hopeless POLICE despite murder, rape and terrorism. Prison population rising due to some other factor than more people being convicted/put in jail, obviously.

CYCLIST - dirty, evil road user who dares to get in the way of cars. A good thing to say about these appalling folk is: "And what about CYCLISTS? All they do is JUMP RED LIGHTS and ride on the PAVEMENT! When will the police crack down on them flouting THE HIGHWAY CODE?!?!? NB cycling is derided no matter if it is a 'friendly' person doing it, e.g. DAVID CAMERON. Cf PEDESTRIAN.

DEATH PENALTY - should be brought back for all crimes that make white people feel scared at night, regardless of true nature of crime.

DEPORTATION - perfectly acceptable call to make on brown criminal, even if born in Britain. Bonus points for "Deport him and his family!"

DOLE - is what scroungers get given to feed their eight billion kids, and guess who's paying?!

ECSTASY - is a drug that kills everyone who takes it straight away.

EXPAT - is the most qualified person to speak about the evils of immigration. Bonus points for saying "They shouldn't let them in" from your computer in a gated villa complex in the Algarve.

FACEBOOK - is an incomprehensible evil that lures children into a seedy world of paedophilia, drugs and prostitution.

FATHER - much maligned 50 per cent of parenthood, deliberately targeted by NuLab and Harriet Harperson so that they will become redundant in 50 years' time. NuLab don't think we need fathers.

FERAL YOUTH - the correct term for anyone under 25.

FEMINISM - appalling stain on humanity caused by uppity women who have had the disgraceful misconception that they deserve to be paid equally and treated the same as men. Should be described as 'man-hating' with pejorative implication of butch lesbianism. Feminists want to kill off men and destroy family units.

GOLLIWOG - harmless teddy for children with no racial connotations whatsoever. Anyone who complains about them is a NULAB PC fascist with 'no sense of humour'.

GREEN ISSUES - that global warming, it's all a con, innit? I saw some programme on Channel 4 once, it's all a myth, nothing's wrong, keep driving our cars and it'll all be fine. We can't affect nature, it's all going to be fine, anything green is just a STEALTH TAX by NU LAB to kill off the TAX PAYER.

GUARDIAN READERS - wilfully ignorant yoghurt-weaving sandal-clad Islington-dwelling fools who want to strangle our babies and kill everyone, bringing a wave of MULTICULTURALISM and LIBERAL values to our ONCE-GREAT COUNTRY.

GYPSIES - criminal, malicious, caravan-dwelling field-desecrators who all have 93 dogs and 125 children (AND GUESS WHO'S PAYING?!?!?!!) and whose sole intention in life is to upset white, MIDDLE CLASS NORMAL PEOPLE by parking their vehicles on open land within 55 miles of them. SCUM, VERMIN and PARASITES.

HARPERSON, HARRIET - Hilarious alternative for Harriet Harman. Evil witch who hates men and wants to destroy the world through political correctness.

HELL IN A HANDCART - phrase that implies that

immigration or liberalism will destroy the bedrock of our society and that doom can only happen in some unspecified time in the future.

IMMIGRATION - secret plot by NU LAB to kill off INDIGENOUS POPULATION by bringing in foreigners, who all smell, are criminals and often terrorists. Every single immigrant is on benefits, and TAXPAYER must foot bill.

INDIGENOUS POPULATION - code for 'white'.

ISLAM - terrorists who want to kill us. Bonus points for using 'religion of peace - I don't think so?!' ironically after a terrorist attack, whether Muslims were involved in it or not.

IT NEVER DID ME ANY HARM - can be used for bullying, beating, torture, any kind of child abuse basically.

I WON'T BE ALLOWED TO SAY THIS - then say it. To give the impression that the PC BRIGADE or communist-infiltrated BBC are somehow denying free speech to the commenter.

JUDGES - Sopping-wet pinko fools who let everyone off crimes and don't give anyone life in prison for stealing a penny bun from a market stall, so are therefore a 'soft-touch' thanks to NU LAB and THE PC BRIGADE.

KILLING - understandable if it's shooting a Brazilian electrician six times in the head; understandable if you're a speeding driver killing a pedestrian; perfectly understandable if you're one of OUR BOYS shooting a brown person.

KNIFE CRIME EPIDEMIC - London-based killings and stabbings in 2008 which, despite being less prevalent than in 2007, are now more prevalent. Pay particular attention to ethnicity of offenders when black, but not when white.

LABOUR WILL TAX IT - useful phrase for any story about anything ever. E.g. rollerskating labrador dog called Simon wins competition. Why not chip in with a hilarious 'LABOUR WILL TAX IT!!!!!'

LIBERALS - scummish, nasty, vile, putrid, disgusting, hateful, fascistic, unpleasant, gay, dirty, disgraceful load of bastards who hate everyone and want everyone to suffer and be miserable, except lesbian one-armed black immigrants. Bonus points for saying "It'd be all right if I was one of them, then the LIBERALS would give me everything I want!"

LITTLEJOHN, RICHARD - hilariously funny, better-than-Proust chronicler of HELL-IN-A-HANDCART PC-GONE-MAD NU LAB bonkers YOU COULDN'T MAKE IT UP Britain.

LOCKED UP - what any criminal or mentally ill person should be. Bonus points for 'and throw away the key!'

MATRON - mythical Hattie Jacques figure who, when re-introduced back into hospitals, will automatically kill off MRSA and clostridium difficile (regardless of fact that matrons still exist in hospitals and their remit includes hygiene). Bonus points for use of "Bring back matron" in smug capital letters or recounting interminably shite story about how you once went into a hospital and there was wee on the toilet seat.

MENTAL ILLNESS - deluded nonsense from milksop LIBERALS who refuse to pull socks up and get on with life as IT NEVER DID ME ANY HARM. Best if all people with such delusions are LOCKED UP to keep them away from NORMAL PEOPLE.

MIDDLE CLASSES - good, kind-hearted, lovely folk who are the best people in the world, especially the white ones, yet who are constantly under attack from STEALTH TAXES and THE PC BRIGADE.

MULTICULTURALISM - must be described as 'failed experiment' (cf SOCIALISM) and be portrayed as reason for all problems everywhere, particularly at times when non-whites have committed crimes.

MUSLIMS - see ISLAM. There are no Muslims other than rabid jihadist murderers - the actions of one extremist Muslim mean, naturally, that every other individual from the same faith is exactly the same as this person.

NATIONAL SERVICE - should be compulsory for everyone younger than me. Never did me any harm! Or the Krays.

NEW LABOUR - A bunch of Stalinist scum who are deliberately killing our children. Please use the correct term 'NuLab'.

NORMAL PEOPLE - anyone with rabidly right-wing views, cf THE SILENT MAJORITY.

NU LAB - is the correct term for 'New Labour'. Can be used as in phrases such as 'Welcome to NuLab Britain, great here isn't it? Thanks a lot Gordie McSporranbotherer!'

OBAMA - Use 'Osama', or if preferred, 'Hussein', to emphasise darkness of skin and therefore evil Islamist tendencies.

ONCE-GREAT COUNTRY - Britain. Used to imply that starving Indians to death and raping other countries was actually the thing we should be proudest of as a nation.

OUR BOYS - correct term for armed forces.

PARASITE - anyone who claims benefits, or any immigrant even if they claim no benefits at all.

PC BRIGADE, THE - Mysterious A-teamesque band of malfaisants who deliberately try to upset white, middle-class heterosexual men by making everyone else have better opportunities as them. Ignore the murderous savages of Islam by their well-intentioned but ultimately evil 'multiculturalism'. Allow murdering chldren to stay in luxury 5-star leisure camps at taxpayer's expense rather than torturing them in barrels of brine, as would be right and proper.

PC GONE MAD - anything which is slightly sensitive

towards other people's cultural traditions or values. Anyone who ever tries to think about other people's feelings is PC GONE MAD and therefore a LIBERAL idiot. See also MULTICULTURALISM.

PEDESTRIAN - foul-smelling creatures who get in the way of cars. Cf CYCLIST

PHILLIPS, MELANIE - world's greatest intellect, a towering lone voice fighting against the terror of MUSLIMS, ISLAM and left-wing idiot GEORGE W BUSH.

POLES - swan-eating miscreants who undercut our Traditional British Plumbers and bring over families of ten trillion children to scrounge off our benefits system... and guess who's paying?!?!

POLICE - either harmless Heartbeat-style 1960s bobbies on bicycles or dirty scum who give you speeding tickets instead of catching 'real criminals', depending on what you're commenting on.

POWELL, ENOCH - visionary titan of brilliance who 'saw it all coming' and first realised the dangers of MULTICULTURALISM's failed experiment as well as the hell of SOCIALISM.

PUBLIC SECTOR - parasitic drain on already overburdened Great British TAXPAYER who, disgracefully, have half-decent pensions (must be described as "gold-plated"). All council workers must be called "diversity officers" who are poisoning our babies with PC GONE MAD views about

MULTICULTURALISM and only offering jobs to one-armed black lesbians.

QUEEN, THE - Her Majesty. Wonderful ruler of Empire. Has regrettably produced rubbish children who will wreck our glittering monarchy.

RANDOM QUOTE FROM SOMEONE WHO SOUNDS AUTHORITATIVE - Try 'But wasn't it Marx himself who said that workers should be boiled alive in tramp sick?' or 'But wasn't it Plato who said that immigration was the worst thing ever?'[10]

REAGAN, RONALD - Benevolent, delightful 'Old Dutch', charming and witty, intellectual giant who spread joy and happiness throughout the world.

RICH, THE - much misunderstood, wonderful wealth generators who are responsible entirely for economic success, but never responsible for economic problems. Kind, gentle, philanthropic people who don't deserve to be taxed at all.

SAVAGES - useful term for anyone living in non-white country or 'Black Africa', who have lived terrible lives since colonial times without white masters to look after them. Important to declare that "We won't bail you out

---

[10] I can't believe I put this in without mentioning Orwell. Orwell is the go-to guy for random quotes in online discussions nowadays.

any more!"

SCUM - anyone who isn't a white, middle-class English Anglo-Saxon taxpayer. And quite a few who are. Cf VERMIN.

SILENT MAJORITY - millions and millions of people who all agree with rabidly right-wing views but don't ever have the courage to express them for fear of upsetting the PC BRIGADE and LIBERALS.

SINGLE MOTHER - PARASITE who has embraced horror of FEMINISM and foolishly decided to live life without man - AND GUESS WHO'S PAYING?!??! Produce FERAL YOUTH who go around committing all crime, unlike nice middle-class children who live in semi-detached houses in Surrey, whose only reason for not committing crime is presence of FATHER.

SMOKING - harmless pastime enjoyed by dignified people who are constantly under attack from PC do-gooders.

SOCIALISM - despicable 'failed experiment' (cf MULTICULTURALISM) which makes everyone miserable. The politics of NULAB, regardless of tax breaks for the rich, tax increases for the poor, etc.

STEALTH TAX - any fine for anything ever, eg speeding ticket, bin being too full. Easily avoided by anyone other than the wilfully stupid, yet still supposedly aimed at MIDDLE CLASSES rather than anyone else, reason never explained.

TAXPAYER - should be prefixed with 'already overburdened'. Mythical chap who pays for immigration, young people, single mums etc and is always on the verge of 'getting fed up about it'.

THATCHER, MARGARET - Kind, gentle, loving old grandmother who was 'the best thing to ever happen to this country'. Smashed evil UNIONS in pay of Colonel Gaddafi and fought off Marxist cell aka Labour Party led by Michael Foot and Neil Kinnock. Supported lovely, decent humanitarian leaders such as PW Botha and Augustin Pinochet as part of her mission to restore pride to this ONCE GREAT COUNTRY. Bonus points for arguing that, because Trotskyite TONY BLAIR embraced privatisation and Thatcherite policies, the 'argument is over' and 'there is no debate'.

UNIONS - appalling 1970s rapists of industry who brought the country to its knees and whose sole purpose in life is to wreck Great Britain. Bonus points for 'Striking won't do you any good, you've got gold plated pensions?! What about me, I don't have a union, I just get on with my job and I love my 0.1 per cent pay rise?!'

VERMIN - handy catch-all phrase which doesn't quite count as downright abuse, so can easily be used to describe gypsies, immigrants or anyone you might disagree with. Cf SCUM.

VIOLENCE - unpleasantness committed by YOUNG PEOPLE and FERAL YOUTH thanks to BINGE BRITAIN. Perfectly acceptable when committed by OUR BOYS in Afghanistan/Iraq.

WINTER - it gets cold, yet this can be seen of evidence that climate change isn't happening. Try using "It's snowing outside my window, ARE YOU WATCHING MR GORE?!!?!"

X-RATED - things that only adults over 75 should be allowed to see, eg a glimpse of a lady's ankle.

YOBS - see FERAL YOUTH. Alternatively use "scrotes" for anyone under 25 who happens to be standing outside a shop.

YOU COULDN'T MAKE IT UP - catch-all Littlejohnian phrase for things which are, as it turns out, frequently actually made up.

YOUNG PEOPLE - See FERAL YOUTH. Are responsible for all crime everywhere ever. Listen to evil music that makes them mad and kill grannies. Should have been disciplined more properly with THE BIRCH and then they wouldn't have turned out this way. But sadly THE PC BRIGADE is in charge of our education and let them off everything.

ZERO TOLERANCE - would solve everything. All children found on streets killed would mean no more yobs bothering our grannies. Being flayed alive for theft would stop all thefts instantly. But will this Government do anything? No they won't!

Fucking Bigtrak

January 27, 2010

And yes, I mean "fucking Bigtrak". If I wanted to say Bigtrak I'd say Bigtrak. But no. I mean fucking Bigtrak. The intensifier is important. I'd even, tmetically, go for "Big-fucking-trak" if "fucking Bigtrak" didn't sound so *right*. As in "What was that little robot thing on wheels that you couldn't afford?" - "Oh, that was *fucking Bigtrak*, thanks for dredging up all those dark memories, you utter bastard.

Yes, Bigtrak is back[11]:

> *Bigtrak was one of the awesomest toys of the 1980s (actually introduced in 1979), and, like other 80s icons, Knight Rider and the A-Team, it is staging a comeback.*

Like other icons of the 1980s which have been resurrected, like Knight Rider and the A-Team, it's going to be a pretty shite shadow of the former glory. (I mean, Val Kilmer doing Kitt's voice? Hello?) One reason for this is quite understandable. *I'm not fucking eight years old any more*[12]. The pleasure of a fucking toy on wheels that you

---

[11] wired.com/gadgetlab/2010/01/bigtrak-is-back-80s-robo-toy-resurrected/

[12] Microsoft Word wants to change this to anymore. I'm not going to let it. Ha ha. In your FACE.

could program to bring you in a can of Coke - yes, it would drive *a fucking can of Coke* from your kitchen to your living room, through the magic of complex programming sequences all punched into its space-age 10-digit keypad, no less - is not the same when you're not a tiny child staring in wonderment at this mass of battery power and plastic struggling to power its way through the shagpile with a weighty Coke can on its robot back, and you are in fact a rather pathetic, tragic-looking old man, who was once an eight-year-old boy who marvelled at the fucking Bigtrak, but whose parents couldn't afford one; or worse, could afford one, but thought it was shit, so got you some fucking Kenny Dalglish football boots for your birthday instead, like that was any fucking kind of substitute - like it was even comparable!

Of course, I have a feeling this new Bigtrak isn't going to be aimed at the kids. It'll be aimed at those beta-male dads who never quite got around to playing with the fucking Bigtrak in the first place, but who now have the disposable income to say: "Do you know what, fuck it. The bills may be piling up and the credit cards may be right on the limit, and the kids may need clothes and lunches and all that shit, but I'm going to buy myself a fucking Bigtrak, because I want one, because I've spent all this time earning money and I want it, so there, and I'll pretend it's for the children, but secretly I'm not going to let them touch it, because it's mine, and it's going to take away all those horrible memories of having to watch the fucking Bigtrak adverts on the TV, knowing deep down that I could never have one, and there would always be a fucking Bigtrak-sized hole in my heart."

Fucking Bigtrak.

Of course, I want one. Oh, I won't lie to you. I want one, all right. I want one now. I want to have one, just because I can. I might buy it just to break it. I might drive the fucking Bigtrak off the side of a bridge, just to punish it for having taunted me throughout primary school. I might program it to drive into the bypass at rush hour, see how the little bastard enjoys that. I might just buy it, just to have it in the box. And then, at Christmas time, I'll wrap it up and stick it under the tree, then look puzzled when I see it there, then unwrap it excitedly and say "YES! Yes! At fucking last! This should have happened twenty-six fucking bastard years ago! Then I'd have fucking well turned out all right! If only I'd had the fucking Bigtrak, everything would have been OK! But no. Oh no! No. No, and now look at me. A broken man on the cusp of middle-age and desperate decline, sending presents to himself and pretending to be surprised, despite having gone to the shop and bought the wrapping paper, and wrapped it, and hidden it at the back of the wardrobe."

Or something like that.

Fucking Bigtrak. Your 'trak' wasn't even that 'big' anyway.

You still haunt me.

I don't like other people earning good money, says man off on luxury holiday[13]

March 21, 2010

A MAN going on a luxury holiday has spoken of his disgust upon hearing that other people want to earn a living wage.

"I mean, I don't want them to be slaves," he said, parking his BMW in a £500-an-hour space at Heathrow. "But a decent wage? Who the hell told them they deserve that kind of thing?

"When I'm on a plane, I want to be served by people who earn considerably less than me. Where is my dignity if they don't? Next you'll be telling me they can afford to have

---

[13] British Airways staff had voted to go on strike against deterioration in pay and conditions. A lot of news articles pointed out that BA staff had relatively good pay and conditions, as if that was somehow some reason why they should just grin and bear it. There were also a lot of vox pops at the time with disgruntled passengers who were dismayed that people should dare to have a democratic ballot to try and improve their working lives. And that's where this came from. People sometimes suggest that I should use better language than things like 'off on', but I like it.

mortgages, or new cars, or stuff like that. I mean, hello? Who's the one with the money here?"

Arthur Bastard, 33, from Hemel Hempstead, continued his tirade against striking British Airways workers as he wheeled his bomb-proof Samsonite luggage towards the first class line to catch a plane to somewhere expensive enough to impress the neighbours and colleagues at work, but which he quite frankly hadn't even heard of a couple of weeks ago.

"I had thought of South Africa," he said, "but I had heard that had become affordable in the past few years. People who shop at Argos being on the same plane as you? Sharing the same air? It's a pretty foul thing."

Bastard had a five-star room booked somewhere ridiculously exotic where a man comes around into your room every three hours and turns over your pillows, makes a nice animal shape out of the bath towels and then puts some tropical flowers on top. But now, like so many others, he faces misery due to the striking workers.

"I heard that at other airlines the workers were paid much less, so that's a good thing. Pay everyone less. Make them suffer. Drag everyone down. Unless of course I'm getting paid more than someone in an equivalent job, in which case I deserve it," grumbled Bastard, accepting a complimentary cut-glass swan of champagne in the Privilege Lounge.

"People who work on aeroplanes... having a decent career?" he frothed. "What good will that do? You don't do that sort of job because of the money, you do it because of the love. And getting free flights just because you work at an airline? Appalling. I was saying to someone serving me an eight-course lunch the other day at our corporate hospitality box at the Emirates that this sort of thing had gone on long enough. And I really think it has. Of course, he chose to say nothing..."

Unlike so many others, whose holidays and possibly lives have been ruined by not getting exactly the flight they wanted to their pampering sun-soaked destination, Bastard was in luck. His flight left on time, but he had one parting shot as a man with a palm-leaf fanned him on his way to the departure gate. "They don't know they're born!" he roared.

"They need to get into the real world."

Gay B&B owner: Let me ban Tories[14]

---

[14] This marked a bit of a change in blogposts, which became a bit more spoofy. As one reader remarked, "like the Daily Mash but without the humour". But still, I ploughed on through. I think I'd reached a point where the whole "Oh look, something a bit crappy in one of the tabloids, look at this!" thing had begun to pall a bit and I felt like I'd taken it as far as I could – and besides, there were (and are) many other bloggers doing that kind of thing far better than I

April 4, 2010

A GAY B&B owner says so-called 'diversity' legislation which prevents him from banning Tories from his hotel is 'political correctness gone mad, or something'.

Dan Jones had a visit from the PC Brigade after refusing to let out a room to a pair of Conservative voters last week.

"Apparently it's something to do with their human rights, or something," fumed Dan, 26. "But I knew what they'd be getting up to in that room: talking about Tory policies all night, free market thinking, discussing privatisation. Maybe even talking about Christianity. It's enough to turn your stomach over. Under my roof! Well I wasn't having any of that."

In yet another example of Bonkers Britain under NuLieBore, Dan says he was then "given a mild rebuke" for kicking the Tory voters down the hallway, punching them in the face and throwing their luggage at their heads.

"You can't do anything nowadays," he simmered. "What kind of country is this today? All I did was beat the crap out of a couple of Tories, and then the police came

---

could. So I decided to try and veer off in a bit of a different direction, for my own amusement as much as anything else. A bit of a bonus was that these posts seemed to be quite popular with readers. Still, I may have lost some original readers from the childish spoofs, too; who knows?

around, saying I wasn't really meant to be allowed to do that kind of thing."

One of the ejected Conservatives, who asked not to be named, said: "Look, no-one at work knows about my lifestyle. It's my choice, I can do what I want. Why shouldn't I be allowed to drone on and on endlessly about National Insurance and what a great chancellor George Osborne would be? Bloody queers. Shit, I mean, er, PC Nazis. Or something. Don't make me sound bad."

We're absolutely fucking clueless, admit football pundits

July 4, 2010

BRITAIN'S football pundits have released a statement condemning their own ignorance and lack of insight, and have offered their immediate resignation.

In a surprise move that echoes the admission of pointlessness expressed by political reporters during the recent general election, the pundits have contributed a joint statement bemoaning their "feeble and tedious" analysis, regretting their "inexcusable lack of knowledge" and "ridiculously limited assessments of teams."

The statement, issued on behalf of all of those chirpy but clueless former professional footballers and their TV presenter friends who have shed not a fucking bit of light on this year's World Cup for British TV viewers, begins: "We, the undersigned, may have tried to give the impression that we knew anything about football, and international football in particular, ahead of this year's World Cup.

"In truth, we now realise that other than watching some Premiership games and maybe the odd bit of La Liga on Sky Sports, we've got no better knowledge that anyone at home. Indeed, anyone with the most rudimentary researching skills probably knows a bit more about world football than we do.

"We had hoped to bluff our way through our crushingly inexcusable ignorance with a bit of chat and some accurate predictions, but since we all smugly sat there and said that a Brazil-Argentina final was almost inevitable, we're a bit fucked when it comes to that fig-leaf, if truth be told.

"Sure, we're ex-professionals, but instead of actually doing our well-paid job and doing some proper research into world football, we just sat around joking about what a funny thing it was that nations like Japan and Paraguay dared to even play football in the first place, as well as patronising all the African teams as much as humanly possible, then expecting that a bunch of players from the English Premiership, the Best League In The World (tm), would find their way into the final, because we'd heard of them.

"We now realise this was not as professional as it could have been.

"Yes, we did some slow-motion replays of goals with

exciting graphics and so on, but this, if anything, exposed our lack of insight all the further. It still didn't shed any light on why one team might be playing better than the other.

"With a heavy heart and after a lot of soul-searching, we now ask that we be relieved of our duties immediately by our employers, and our salaries given instead to some bloke from down the pub called Jeff who's actually heard of players outside the Premiership and understands that there are leagues in Europe and South America as well as the famous ones."

A BBC spokesman added: "We did think that viewers appreciated these millionaires being flown out to South Africa and not doing even the most basic of research for their well-paid jobs, but apparently, for some reason, they don't."

An ITV insider said: "Look, we've got the best theme music and some nice graphics. We've blown the rest of the budget on Moon Face Chiles so there wasn't any cash for people who'd actually bothered to fucking learn something about international football. You'll just have to make do with shit like Chris Coleman, all right?"

Why do I love my ironing board?

August 20, 2010

Ironing boards have quite an important meaning for me. I don't particularly like ironing in itself - though there's something therapeutic about reducing the creases in a piece of fabric, or seeing a wrinkly bit of material become flattened and reduced to smooth cloth through the magic of steam and heat; of course there is - but I do like the equipment.

I know this may sound slightly odd. I appreciate that. But I find a certain sense of comfort when I see an iron, or an ironing board*. Particularly the ironing board, more than the iron; though just the sight of an iron can be enough, in itself. It often depends on the mood I'm in at the time. If I'm more gloomy than is normally the case, I may need to actually put up the ironing board and do some ironing on it before the darkness fades away like so much steam into a piece of flaxen cloth.

No matter. I think it has something to do with the patterns - those majestic swirls of colour, those jarringly overexcited oranges and lime greens, those daring blobs of purple and teal - although I'd be the first to admit that you can get plain ones as well. (Don't let me be caught out twice in a week claiming that things are only available in a patterned variety when there are indeed literally dozens of plain options available! No, I've learned my lesson, all right.)

They're part of the reason, but there's something else as well - an ironing board is something that doesn't really belong in any room. When erected, it stands there almost apologetically, dangling the flex of the iron over the side like a stray trail of sputum or something lazily drooling out of its mouth; when folded up, it's still somehow out of place, all the time, unless you come across it wedged between cardboard boxes and bits of polystyrene in a cupboard somewhere, or hanging from the back of a door (I'm aware that some people have hooks that they like to hang their ironing boards from).

There's the sound of it, as well, somewhere between what you might imagine a medieval torture device would sound like slicing off someone's genitals and the more reassuring clunk of a car door being slammed, as it locks into place. Whenever I try and open/close the one at home, the cat inevitably goes scuttling out of the room, fearing imminent death. It's not unusual for my cat, who has a terrific fear of death from almost every single everyday activity you can think of, but it would appear there's something particularly fearful about the ironing board. That's strange, because I find there's something particularly pleasant about it.

What I like most about my ironing board, though - and it's important that we're talking about my ironing board, as opposed to ones I might use in hotel rooms or in someone else's house, for example - is the sense that I plucked it, many years ago, from Argos, and brought it home with me. Looking back, it's probably one of the first things I ever bought when I left home for good and wandered out into adulthood, blinking and somewhat confused, all those years ago. I remember lumbering back to the miserable place I used to live with it tucked under my arm, thinking, well, I've got an ironing board.

As well as that, in the same way that some people have teddy bears as transitional objects that have seen them through the years and psychologically replaced the mother-child bond, I've got my slightly grubby orange-and-green ironing board. I remember sitting as a child watching my mother doing the ironing, thinking something which had been explained as so *dangerous* must be a very adult task to do. When I bought my own ironing board, it was a way of trying to grow up a bit and carry on those things I'd learned as a child, how to try and be tidy, how to try and iron things out, and so on.

The irons seem to wear out more often than the ironing board does. I had to buy one the other day - sat in Argos, waiting for my order to come around, I realised I was at that magical moment when order 999 had been called, and now we were in new territory. I'd never been there during the reboot before, but there it was - all of a sudden we were back to order number 001. There is no 000, I discovered, and I suppose that only makes sense. I was 006, though, not 001 or 002, but I didn't mind too much. Another iron to use on the ironing board; another trip to Argos to sit around on a little plastic chair and wait for your number to be called.

And I know that when I get home this evening, and everything else might fall apart, that the ironing board, 11 years and still going strong, is still there. As it should be. My ironing board, the thing I can rely on - the constant in my life, when everything else changes.

That's why I love my ironing board. I hope you love yours too.

* If you have yet to read the most marvellous autobiography of all time, and I feel also embarrassed about having to tell you that it's this, if you haven't seen it or experienced its wonders just yet, then you will not have encountered the marvellous couple of sentences about

ironing boards (and lawnmowers) therein. It would be wrong of me not to acknowledge that as an influence on this blog post.

Towards a sensible biscuit hierarchy

September 1, 2010

I've written about biscuits before, specifically Tunnock's wafers. But it was this [Twitter] exchange earlier that reminded me that, in all of our minds, there is a hierarchy of biscuits:

@antonvowl – Yeah, I'm having a fucking Hob-Nob.

@SuziCre – screw your hob nob, I've got Jaffa Cakes aplenty here.

She's right, of course. Jaffa Cakes beat Hob-Nobs, there's no sensible debate to be had there*. Jaffa Cakes win. But it got me thinking. Exactly where do Jaffa Cakes, and Hob-Nobs for that matter, fit in the biscuit hierarchy? If you were playing biscuit poker, a pair of Viscounts would clearly defeat a Rich Tea. *But what about a Trio, or a Taxi?* And how to separate out all those different varieties of Club?

That's where you come in. I'm going to try and establish a rough framework here in this post, but I'm bound to make mistakes. There are some rules - generally biscuits are higher up the food chain if they have a wrapper, particularly a shiny one; and of course, the addition of chocolate improves anything. Now, you may well disagree, but I'm just trying to get things rolling. Feel free to add your own suggestions.

1. Viscounts. Orange or mint. I'm not fussy. All right. I am - make it orange. And bring the fuckers here, right now. I know this may be controversial, but I'm going for Viscounts. I used to call them Viss-counts when I was a kid. What the fuck did I know?

2. Tunnock's Wafers. Of course. How can you go wrong? Lovely pink-and-gold wrappers only hint at the wafer-caramel joy beneath.

3. Choco Leibniz. The ruthlessly efficient Teutonic teatime treat. Shitloads of chocolate are the key here, but you're only getting the kind of flimsy biscuit you'd normally associate with a Choc Dip. Still, nice writing on the back, you can't knock that.

4. Kit-Kats. I'm talking in particular about the Peanut Butter Kit-Kat chunky, although as many of you are aware, there's a whole myriad of different Japanese Kit-Kats[15]. The elusive wasabi Kit-Kat is kind of the Holy Grail there, I'm pretty sure. Wasabi... and Kit-Kat... in one handy biscuit? Oh yes! Points down for it no longer being

---

[15] jenkenskitkatblog.blogspot.com/ - a tremendous treasury of all things Japanese and Kit-Kat related.

in foil that got stuck in your fillings and made you hit the ceiling like you were licking a 9v battery.

5. Clubs. More specifically, the raisin ones. Do they still do them? I mean, fuck the ordinary chocolate ones. Too biscuity, not enough fun. Stick raisins in there, though, and you've got something great.

6. Jaffa Cakes. You may find it surprising they're here at all; you may be surprised they're not higher up. Jaffa Cakes are moreish, of course, but there's something too spongey about them. The smashing jaffa orangey bit is, as far as I'm aware, slightly less smashing than it used to be, as well. You may well have travelled overseas and found Jaffa Cakes will all kinds of delightful fillings - the strawberry, the lime, all kinds of joy - but the orange is the original and still the best.

7. Tuc. Shit name for a biscuit (is it tuck? took? TUC?) and this is a savoury, not a sweet. But you can forgive these little blighters that. Slight problems with the crackers splintering away from the cheesy fondant centre, but apart from that, a tremendous all-rounder.

8. Bourbons. Ah yes. There are only two sensible ways of eating a Bourbon: a) remove one biscuit finger from two separate Bourbons, then place them together for one enormous chocolate-cream filling of wonderment, or b) get rid of one biscuit finger then scrape off the good stuff with your teeth. No other ways are permissable, I'm afraid.

9. Wagon Wheels. You may regard these as being beyond biscuits, but I think they still count. As a child, they seemed to last a few seconds. Now, I probably wouldn't be able to eat more than an eighth of one without being sick all over the floor. There's something satisfying, though, about a biscuit that's so fucking vast that you can't even get it in your mouth.

10. Jammy Dodgers. In a lot of ways, you could see the 'dodger' as the impertinent cousin of the Wagon Wheel, but without the mallow. The jam appears to be some kind of red melted glass suitable for road surfacing, capable of ripping apart even the most elaborate dentistry, and the biscuit itself isn't amazing. But still. It's a bloody jammy dodger.

11. Custard Creams. The baroque engraving on the side of the biscuit, the satisfying crunch-squelch-crunch of the texture, the sheer opulence of the little fuckers. You can dunk these and keep them intact, no worries.

12. Gypsy Creams. Goodness me. These take me back to my childhood, maybe about five years old, when I first started experiencing feelings that made me feel a bit strange. The first time I noticed this was watching Kate Bush doing Babooshka on Top of the Pops, thinking to myself "I don't know why, but I feel a bit weird." Another one to chalk away under 'first stirrings' was the lady in the Gypsy Creams advert, all 80s glistening hair and backlighting, riding a pony or something. It didn't have much to do with gypsies. But ooh. (I'm pretty sure I didn't make this up. Can anyone confirm this actually happened?)

13. Garibaldi. Seriously, this is my crack cocaine. I can't just have one bit. Sure, you can break a bit off and pretend that's all you're going to eat, but then all of a sudden it's half an hour later, and you're covered in crumbs and bits of raisin, and are the approximate size of a small house. For this reason, though, I can't buy Garibaldi any more. Which is a shame.

14. Party rings. These toroid nuggets of sugary love offer the doughnut experience without a doughnut - more two-dimensional, yet still garishly pink and yellow in colour, with a hole in the middle so you can play hoopla with the cat's tail. Not that I'd do that with my cat, as I'd get my face ripped off.

15. Chocolate Hob-Nobs. Of course, chocolate makes anything better. But Hob-Nobs still lurk down the lower reaches.

16. Taxis. Promised so much, didn't it, the Taxi. Ooh, I'm in Manhattan, in a yellow cab, about to bump into Woody Allen. No! It's just a bog-standard biscuit, very little to enjoy here, but hey, it could be worse.

17. Penguins. Nice pictures of penguins on the wrappers, mind.

18. Malted Milk. To be quite blunt, if it weren't for the stencil on the side, I wouldn't touch these fuckers at all.

19. Hob-Nobs. The trouble with dunking these crumbly little jokers is that you end up with separation in your tea, and a resultant oaty sludge in your final couple of mouthfuls. Danger here[16].

20. Chocolate Digestives. The plain chocolate are clearly the important ones here. Don't fuck me around with Cadbury's muddy sludge on there.

Unranked: Nice biscuits (they clearly are *nothing* of the sort).[17]

You may well disagree with these selections, but bear in mind we've all got favourites. Where, for example, is the Blue Riband? In the fucking bin where it belongs, is my answer. But you may be dismayed by that attitude.

* I realise that some of you may not regard Jaffa Cakes as cakes and not biscuits. But for the purposes of the biscuit hierarchy, a 'biscuit' is something (generally) disc-shaped snack you eat, often with a cup of tea, with the approximate diameter slightly smaller than a normal-sized mug, for dunking purposes. I realise that not all biscuits fit this description - the Tunnock's wafer, for example, or the Choco Leibniz. But you get the general idea. Jaffa Cakes,

---

[16] Some of you may have spotted this as a reference to legendary ITV Sport football commentator Brian Moore.

[17] This is one of the most controversial assertions you can make, I have subsequently discovered. Fans of the coconut soi-disant 'Nice' biscuit are pretty vehement in their love.

yes; pork pies, no[18].

The clearly correct definitive list of animals beginning with O

September 13, 2010

I know that the post 'Towards a sensible biscuit hierarchy' attracted a huge wave of controversy, and I feel that this may well do the same. But I couldn't let it rest.

This article in today's Graun, entitled 'Why do we love owls so much?'[19] is what sparked everything off, and I was encouraged to do this list by @Bat020. And sure, I love owls as much as the next man - in fact I know a cracking owl sanctuary not far from here - but that isn't the whole story. There are other creatures, beginning with the letter O, that are just as interesting, if not more so. True, those owls - one could label them the tarts of the bird world, but

---

[18] This was further confused to me on a recent trip to France when I saw the French version of Jaffa Cakes labelled quite clearly on the packet as 'biscuits'. So there. Make whatever you want out of that, I'm saying nothing.

[19] www.guardian.co.uk/theguardian/2010/sep/12/why-do-we-love-owls

I'm not unkind - sit there with their big eyes and their beaks and their giant circular faces and all of that, and, yes, owls flap about and have big wings. But don't tell me that they're better than otters, because they *aren't.*

So, here is the definitive list, completely correct and impossible to argue against, of animals beginning with the letter O. I think you'll find that everything is in order - but if you do happen to have your own views on the subject, feel free to join in with the disgruntled masses in the comments box.

1. Otters. Obviously. Was it an owl that got its head pummeled into a meaty pulp by that bloke with a spade at the end of Ring of Bright Water? I think not. Would we have cried as much? A bit, but not as much as the cute little otter. Look, otters are fucking brilliant. Don't fuck with me on this one, because you know they are. Sea otters, freshwater otters, short-clawed otters, Asian otters, European otters - face it, they're the pinnacle of O-animals. Look at their little faces! Look at their little paws! Look at the fact they gnawed off Terry Nutkins's fingers! Look at all of it! They even make little squeaky noises like Sweep. I once went to an otter sanctuary where the keeper told me: "I know we shouldn't feed them this, but they really love chips." *They love chips as well.* You want more? OK, here's more:

Oh yes. From the splendid cute baby otters website (Ronseal: It's a website full of cute baby otters) - courtesy of Bellamack.

2. Ocelots. In many ways one could claim that the ocelot is merely a small big-cat or a big small-cat, but that would be to ignore the ears. I mean, the eyes! *Look at the fucking eyes!*

3. Orangutans. It says something about the wondrousness of ocelots and otters that orangutans, the spectacular ginger apes, are only in position number 3. Many people delight in the sight of the baby orangutan, a tiny ball of orange fluff, but for me the older ones are even better.

They're critically endangered as well, these poor little russet-coloured blighters, through no fault of their own[20].

4. Owls. Obviously, they were going to turn up. And yes, there are many reasons why the owls are traditionally thought of as wise old birds - the giant faces, the big eyes, the silly half-asleep Stewie Griffin faces, the rotating heads, and all of that. I like them because they have that combination of expression between "I am the slightest bit peeved" and "I couldn't give a flying fuck" on their faces. Do you know what I mean? I think this picture sums it up nicely:

(Imagine a picture of an owl)[21]

---

[20] I have been lucky enough to see orangutans in the wild. I've even been attacked by one. Probably the best thing ever.

[21] Isn't that lazy of me? 'Imagine a picture of an owl'. But obviously this book has words, and not pictures. Imagine an owl, go on. A scary, angry-looking owl face. No, angrier than that. That's it.

And that comes from the marvellous Fuck You, Penguin blog[22].

5. Octopuses / Octopodes / Octopi / Whatever the fuck you want to call them. These leggy submariners have the added bonus of being not only interesting animals, but also delicious. Which is bad for them, obviously, but not bad for Greek restaurants. Several new species of octopus have recently been discovered, including this joker:

(Imagine a picture of an octopus that looks quite jolly. A nice pink happy octopus, maybe a bit like a pink elephant. Something like that. There, you can almost see it in your mind's eye, can't you? How could you eat such a thing? How could you? You couldn't, that's the answer. You couldn't, and you know you couldn't.)

I don't think I could eat him, he looks like he might be quite fun. Unless he's *really* delicious, in which case I probably would.

Not ranked - ostriches. Scary, stary little bleeder, the ostrich. Just stands there with that unfeasibly long neck, forever on the verge of pecking your eyes out or headbutting you. Nasty. *shudders*

So, those are my top five, and clearly correct though they are, you may have your own views. NB taxonomical

---

[22] www.fupenguin.com/2009/04/jaded-hipster-owls-think-theyve-seen-it.html

corrections are only relevant if you understand that my definition of 'animal' is "thing that's alive and isn't a plant, or fungus, or something".

Wrestling, football and immigration

September 6, 2009

This thoughtful post by Left Outside[23] on the coverage given to immigration in the papers has got me thinking. At times in the past I've thought of the press as deliberately giving their readers a scare, like a rollercoaster ride or a Ghost Train, tapping into that primitive fight-or-flight part that makes you pleased to have the adrenalin pumping around your bloodstream: Whoooh look, the bogeyman! And you run away and hide behind the settee, then are relieved to find out that everything's OK, that your Muslim neighbours aren't plotting to bomb your house, that thousands of Poles haven't yet streamed into your street, that life isn't as scary as you might have been led to believe.

I wonder if there isn't something different going on,

---

[23] leftoutside.wordpress.com/2009/09/06/migration-is-not-a-crime-but-the-way-its-discussed-is-criminal/

though. It struck me while watching England's tedious football friendly against Slovenia yesterday that commentators are more often than not pretty nonsensically partisan when the national team's in action - or even when 'our' club sides are taking on Johnny Foreigner in the Champions League or whatever. We have eyes and we can see when fouls are committed and when players take to the ground like a sack of spuds that's been dumped off the back of a van - yet the commentators try and tell us that we haven't seen what we've seen. When Wayne Rooney, for example, kicks another player in the shins, we're expected to believe that he hasn't done it; or when one of 'our' lads goes stacking into the turf at a great rate of knots under a powder-puff challenge we're expected to think that it hasn't happened.

Partisan commentators want us to think in terms of heroes and villains. We can't have the narrative being one in which both England and opposition players are equally capable of searing fouls or dirty cheating dives; it has to be implied that those 'continental' shysters are somehow more naughty at cheating than our brave battlers - that our boys get stuck in and play honestly, whereas the sly tricksters from overseas are always trying to con the ref with feigning injury and plummeting to the ground, things that 'we' would never do. (It's even more bizarre to see this kind of commentary played out on those occasions when an English team made up of immigrants - French, Spanish, Ivory Coast, whatever - takes on an Italian, or French, or Spanish team made up of immigrants. Of course English boys would never feign injury or dive or cheat or foul - and neither would our adopted heroes!)

I was thinking at the time of why football commentators frequently spin these silly narratives about matches, when the fans can see in very stark terms that that isn't what's going on. They can see English players cheat, dive and foul all game long, and they know it's happening. Sure, they roar their disapproval when the other side do it, but that's the way it is. That's the part you have to play. I don't know whether it makes as much sense for commentators to make out that English players are always angels and those foreign types are always out to cheat their way to victory, since they're meant to be telling you what's happening rather than what you'd like to be happening - but then maybe that is their role?

Maybe if you just saw it with your eyes you wouldn't be as patriotic about it? Maybe if you didn't have the bellowing voice of Peter Drury, John Motson or whoever telling you that we're getting a raw deal because we're playing fair you wouldn't enjoy it as much? I don't know. All I do know is that England have cheated as well as the best of them down the years. Sometimes you get away with it and sometimes you don't, but I think everyone does it.

And then I thought about wrestling. The world of wrestling has always (in this country at least) been divided into 'blue-eyes' and 'heels', those characters you're there to cheer for and those you're meant to boo to the rafters (especially when they're cheating behind the referee's back!), and the lines are fairly delineated. It's important for the theatre of the whole thing, and it doesn't work otherwise. Just a couple of blokes chucking each other around a ring isn't as entertaining as one guy who's going to try and cheat his way to victory, conning the oblivious referee who always happens to be looking the wrong way in the process, fighting against someone else who's going to play fair. That's the set-up, and that's how you react as a participant in the theatre, as a ringside spectator: roaring your disapproval at the unfairness of it all.

A friend of mine once told a story of going to all-in wrestling as a child, when it was at its peak of popularity, and seeing two guys going at each other like they really hated each other in the ring, like there was a real feud going on between them. Then being shocked and disappointed afterwards to see them laughing at joking at the bar. All that anger he'd screamed from the audience seemed entirely wasted.

Which brings me to the newspapers and to immigration. The story they tell is no more real than the one the football commentators would have you believe, and no more real than the tableaux acted out in the wrestling ring. But it presses the same buttons. Not those that spark fear, so much, but those which prompt outrage; those which make you demand justice against a lack of fairness.

Immigration stories are, as Left Outside points out, fairly commonly fitting into a template of sorts. Generally we are led to believe that we are being overwhelmed by too many immigrants, that those immigrants are stealing British jobs, that if they aren't doing that they're going to the front of the housing queue and siphoning off benefits from what our friends at the BNP would call the 'indigenous' population, that whatever they're doing that some of them are here to commit murder in the name of their savage religion; and, above all, that it's all either (a) tacitly accepted by the Government in order to bring in cheap labour or even (b) actively encouraged because for some reason they think that all immigrants/Muslims/whatever will vote in their favour.

That's where the rage comes from. The referee's looking the wrong way! He's been conned by the heels! He's been deceived by those chippy foreigners! And there's nothing we can do about it except holler from the stands!

Except it's not true. I've said many times before that I don't know whether people really care whether these immigration stories are true or not. What they want is that chance to rant, to roar, to shout and scream about what they reckon is unfair.

Which would be fine if the Mail and Express and the others marketed their stories as being like wrestling - you know and I know what's going on, but let's just enjoy ourselves in the heat of the rage for a half-hour or so. But they don't: they market themselves as the tellers of truths and the people who reveal what is really going on. That's where the difference comes. You can scoff at a bit of biased football commentary and think, ah well, I guess it's all about creating a bit of heat and light; and you can shrug your shoulders at a bit of wrestling - it's a bit of fun, and the outrage quickly dies down.

But telling lies about immigrants is something entirely different. It creates that feeling of rage, gets the hackles up and creates a splutter for the spectators, in this case your readers. But it's fundamentally dishonest, and unfair, and needs to be dismantled. If you want to get angry over something, get angry over a football match, or over some real injustices. Because this kind of lying leads to aggression, to hatred, to prejudice and in extreme cases to violence. And it's not a bit of fun; it's deadly serious.

News about dicks

February 21, 2010

Dicks[24] sell papers. News about dicks might not be as important as, say, news about real things happening somewhere, but dicks sell papers. You have to bear this in mind.

Take Tiger Woods. Yeah, fine. Second most successful golfer in history. Talented sportsman. But... when he stopped swinging his golf club and started swinging his dick, it all become much more important. All of a sudden it was a real story. Who wants to read about some dull guy plodding up and down a bit of mown grass in a brightly coloured jumper? I mean, hello! But using his dick, to do the things with his dick that dicks are designed to do...? Ah. Now that's public-interest news at its finest. Yes, he has a dick. Yes, he does dick-things with his dick. He uses his dick to have sex with. He probably uses it to have a piss with as well, though we don't have any independent clarification of that. But that's not the interesting thing to do with a dick, is it?

Not a massive revelation, you might imagine, given that the continued existence of the human race proves that

---

[24] I like the word dick, especially as a term of abuse. I also love the phrase uttered by Murray Hewitt in Flight of the Conchords: "a taste of your own dick medicine." Imagine that said in a slightly peeved Kiwi accent. Perfection.

quite a lot of men know how to use their dicks - ah, but, you see, it's all about money. Money and dicks. He has a lot of money, and he has a dick, therefore his dick is more important to know about than, say, my dick or your dick, or, if you don't have a dick - and you're probably better off in so many ways if you don't - someone else's dick. His dick and his sponsorship deals are inextricably linked. If his dick doesn't do what it's supposed to do, that money doesn't go to him. Money and dicks. That's the real story here. How doing the wrong thing with your dick can lead to you losing millions of dollars. It's a dick lottery. It's a big one-dicked bandit. Pull the dick and see if you're a winner.

Tiger started this latest wave of dickmania off in the papers. Dicks have existed since time immemorial, but there was so much interest in his dick and what he'd done with it, that it began to create a big Tiger/dick monster that sold a hell of a lot of papers and got a lot of clicks on the web. There were, it turned out, only a finite number of women who had experienced Tiger's dick, but no matter: thankfully there are a lot of other dicks in the world, and quite a lot of them belong to men with money.

Money and dicks. Bear that in mind, because that's the justification: this man, with a dick, doesn't want you to know about what he does with his dick, and he's got money, and it's probably because he's worried about his sponsorship deals, really. I mean who doesn't want everyone to know what they and their dick get up to? None of the rest of us mind, do we? It must be all about the money. And therefore, by revealing John Terry, or Ashley Cole, or Tiger Woods, or whoever, as someone who does stuff with his dick, the papers are actually exposing them as a hypocrite, and the public have a right to know because *imagine if you bought a fucking razor but you hadn't realised that the man advertising it had done something with his dick you might not approve of*, what then? How can we possibly make informed brand choices without knowing the status of the dick of all the men involved in recommending these products to us? What if their dicks have done stuff we don't think they should have done, but we didn't know because the press weren't there to tell us? We could be buying all sorts of replica sporting equipment or bottles of brown sauce and using all kinds of consultancy firms and stuff... and there where would our lives be?

Dicks sell papers. Not just crappy papers, the ones we laughably dismiss as tabloids. Dicks sell the big boys' papers too, although they pretend that they're merely reporting on the media storm which already exists, and which was nothing to do with them. How can they ignore it, they ask, and shrug. I don't know. Maybe nothing else is going on in the world. I mean it's not as if there's a war or anything, with dozens of innocents being scooped off the roadside with shovels all the time, is it? It's not as if soldiers from this country are coming home in zip-up bags every week, is it? No, the activities of dicks are the only important things out there.

It may only be me. I know a lot of people really do see these things as being important. And I feel I must at this point explain that I don't want stories about dicks banned. You say that you disagree with anything nowadays and someone will tell you you've tried to ban it. No, not banned. I just wish that newspapers were grown-up enough to not give a shit about dicks. I wish we were grown-up enough not to give a shit about dicks. I wish we were more interested in things other than dicks. But what do I know? It would appear that we are obsessed with the bloody things. We're a nation of people giggling in the shower.

You could say it's news about dicks, written by dicks, and read by dicks.

Alex Higgins[25]

July 25, 2010

Some people will tell you that when Gazza broke down in floods of tears in Italia 90, it changed everything. It might have done for a lot of people, but I remember something before then: Alex Higgins's tears when he won the 1982 World Snooker final.

It's hard to separate one moment out of a sporting great's life and say there, that is who the person was, because it's all too easy to slip into the world of cliché, to imagine that everything was perfect before the world titles and there was some inevitable arc towards destruction and eventual death; it's easy to look back and imagine the dots got joined together by straight lines, but you have to suspect that things are even more complicated with Higgins than with anyone else. Here was someone who was quite rightly

---

[25] Alex Higgins died on July 24 after a long battle with cancer.

loved and hated, who acted appallingly and brilliantly. How can you separate it all out? How can you take one strand and say, this is who this person was? It's impossible.

There was always something of the outsider about Higgins. There was a look on his face of a man who'd been wronged, who wasn't quite right, who was always going to have to fight just to stand still. He was more crumpled, more battered, less together than the other neat and tidy snooker stars on television in the 1980s. Higgins didn't wear a tie, citing medical reasons. He'd sit there, screwing his mangled features up as he lit another cigarette, looking like everything could fall apart at any second... but then sometimes it didn't fall apart. Sometimes it all came together.

Higgins was the loser's hero, the guy who couldn't be relied upon to get anything right, but who could, when he did get it right, beat anyone. There's something almost childish about the risk-taking behaviour, the desire to try anything to try and win, to go for the near impossible when the safe option is there, but when it comes off, it's amazing. The more methodical sporting heroes - in snooker, Steve Davis or Ray Reardon - are always going to win more times with their approach. But in this bit of action from 1982, Higgins pulls off an amazing series of shots to crush Jimmy White:

Maybe there's a part of all of us who are failures, and losers, and defeated, who admire the courage of Higgins to go for it when the odds were against him. Those of us who are never going to amount to anything can look at someone like that and think, well, that's what happens when you really try, it might come off, and you might just do it. We all just want a millionth of what he had, and we'd be happy. Here was someone who was a fighter - against his rivals, against authority figures, against cancer, against everyone, including himself, of course. It was that battling spirit that saw him overcome cancer, though the operations and treatment, as well as the lifestyle he'd had, did for him in the end. But he raged against the dying of the light, like he'd raged against everything.

It's hard to like someone like Higgins, whatever you think of his sporting achievements. I dare say in real life he could be an awful person. I don't want to read all the stories from friends and lovers that will no doubt appear in the papers, but I imagine there will be some unsavoury stories that come out - those, after all, are the ones that attract the most attention, the bigger headlines, the potentially bigger payout. Who knows what really happened.

But I just remember being a younger person, looking at Higgins's face contorted in tears as he won that 1982 final. Tears of joy, that he could have won again, despite everything. Tears of relief, that it was all over. And probably tears for all kinds of other reasons, too. Here was someone so painfully, obviously fallible, and yet, there he was, champion of the world, best of everyone. He was a terrible ambassador for the sport, hounded for every tiny swear, cough, indiscretion and so on by the press, often rightly so, sometimes making a lot out of a little. But for those moments, as the tears fell, he was proven to be the best of the best. The rest of us can only dream of such magic. That's why a lot of us love sport, for the power to transport you to somewhere else, to see a glimpse of someone else's dream, to see a part of your own hopes invested in someone else.

And years later, they're gone, and you're still here. But still. If you could have a millionth of what they had, you'd take it right away. I know I would.

I'm not an expert, but… this is why I don't buy newspapers any more[26]

August 8, 2010

I used to like newspapers. Really. I loved them. When I was growing up, we always had newspapers around - my parents thought they'd be useful in teaching their kids to read. And I suppose they were, a bit. We had all sorts - the Sun, the Mail, the Times, never really the Telegraph or the Guardian or anything like that. I always used to read the local paper when it came through the letterbox - primarily to see if anything had happened in places I'd heard of rather than places I could only imagine (it usually hadn't,

---

[26] This was one of a series of posts in which I, as a non-expert, attempted to write some stuff about the media. It was me trying to get a bit more serious and less jokey about what I was blogging, to try and make things a little more considered and less shouty. In some ways I think I succeeded and this was to pave the way for more considered, longer, less sweary and possibly more interesting pieces.

but such is life in dreary cookie-cutter suburbia).

When I was at university I think I started buying the Guardian because that's kind of what you're meant to do when you're a student, but I did enjoy reading it as well. Well, bits of it. And I think I'd get the Independent and the Times as well, or Telegraph when I wanted to read some sport, and News of the Screws on a Sunday for something a bit different, and the unintentional hilarity of the Michael Winner column of course. When I started working, I moved on to the Mirror, which I liked, and then, well that was about it.

I don't buy newspapers any more. I was at the garage this morning going to buy some milk and bread and thought *Why not get a paper*? But then I looked at the bloody things, and I thought: *Actually, I know why not.* What do I want to find out about? Well, some news. All the news in the paper is going to be out of date. There might be a couple of columns that are relevant to stuff that I'm interested in, but there's no guarantee that I'm going to agree with them - which isn't a problem, but if you find yourself disagreeing with columnists more often than you do agreeing with them, why are you buying the paper in the first place?

Sportswise, I want to find out about my team, and I have no interest in Premiership transfers that haven't happened yet, or Premiership players saying they'd like to score goals and win games, and Premiership managers saying they want to win more games than they lose, and all the other obvious banality - but in a newspaper you're going to be lucky if your team - unless it's Liverpool, Arsenal, Manchester United or Chelsea - gets more than three or four paragraphs, sometimes even less than that;

sometimes you're just shunted into the 'round-up' bits. Why bother with that at all?

The thing is, time after time, in every section, you're faced with a tsunami of guff about stuff you're not interested in, just in case you might be interested in it, and the bits you actually are interested in seem tiny in comparison. With Sunday papers it's even worse - there are entire sections immediately consigned to the recycling bin without ever needing to be touched. Sure, it's great value to have so much stuff for such a relatively small price; but on the other hand, it's not great value at all when you don't actually want all the crap you're being given. It gets to the point where you've ploughed through half a ton of flabby lifestyle marketing bollocks about stuff you can't ever possibly afford or ever even have the faintest dream of being able to afford, just to get to the fucking TV guide and the cartoons.

But there's something else. Reading Sunday papers, especially the Sunday 'quality' papers, makes me sad. It makes me feel like a failure. I don't really buy into the whole social Veblenism of it, to try and buy into the whole idea that some holiday on a gold-plated yacht in the middle of the Bahamas eating quails' brains carved into the shape of exploding fireworks off the back of a diamond-encrusted flamingo is really going to be something that I could ever even aspire to, let alone get anywhere near to if I saved up all my money ever. I can't be fucked with looking at half-a-grand's worth of handbag, or shoes, or whatever it is, thinking that is anything to do with my life or has anything whatsoever to do with me. It makes me pissed off. What the fuck has this got to do with me? Page after page of luxury cars that I've not got a rat's chance in hell of ever being able to crash into, let alone buy. It's like MTV Cribs - it just makes me feel shit about my own life, rather than having any of the magic rubbing off onto me. Oh look, someone else marvellously wealthy and with loads of shit that they've bought. Oh look, another home cinema. Fucking magic. Ooh, a big marble bathtub. Good for you. It gets a bit wearying after a while.

It's funny but I don't feel so overwhelmed by the dozens of choices I don't like when I'm thinking of something like broadcasting, for example. The BBC offers loads of programmes that I'm never going to watch, whereas on the other hand it offers a significant proportion of things that are absolutely delightful, and which I enjoy very much. (ITV, in comparison, is just loads of stuff I don't like and am never going to watch. But that's just me.) But I don't feel overwhelmed by it at once. I can pick and choose things as the day progresses, or using the iPlayer. I don't have to constantly turn page after page after page of stuff that I don't like, reading column after column that I find annoying or grating, chucking supplement after supplement into the bin.

Like a lot of people, I feel quite liberated by not having a newspaper any more. I might scan one if there's one knocking about, of course, but it's not something that I go out and buy. In fact, those times when I do just pick up a newspaper remind me why I don't buy them any more - there's so much there that's not for me, so little that I find myself agreeing with or enjoying. Sometimes you'll read an entire newspaper just for a crossword or a TV review. Is that enough? I don't know. It's a lot of effort to put in as a reader for not very much back. I don't think it's the cost that puts me off, I think it's the fact that I don't really enjoy what's in there, and I can seek out any number of entertaining reads online. That's just me, and I know it's very different for other people.

I'm not saying that it's a good thing that people don't buy newspapers any more, because I know it's an industry that often provides very important challenges to Government. There are occasional moments of brilliance that you probably don't get anywhere else, in any other medium. But I can't keep on chucking a quid away every day in the hope that somewhere down the line something good turns up. Maybe that's a selfish attitude, but it's the one I have. I love reading, but I don't love reading newspapers any more. I don't think they've got significantly worse, but maybe I've become more impatient with them, more demanding, more easily annoyed. Or maybe it's the case that there are more readily available sources of reading material and entertainment.

I know that a lot of people will say "You'll miss them when they're gone" and I probably will, or would. But I can't see myself starting to buy them again any time soon.

Snot

September 27, 2010

I write this now because my own olfactory outpourings have turned into blobby pistachio blancmange on the translucent tissue on my computer keyboard. It's late, I'm tired, I'm over the half-life of the Lemsip capsules and, in general, my nose feels like it's been gently sandpapered for the past 18 hours. I've got a fucking cold. I have the kind of rattiness that even falafel can't shift. And you know that means real trouble.

I've tried Berocca - which would be somewhat more appetising were it not that 'first piss of the day' colour - and I have tried oranges. I have eaten fruit and I have eaten stodge. I have tried everything to halt this cold in its tracks.

And yet, the snot keeps coming. An unstoppable tide. A giant dangling polymer of goo. An explosion of nose jizz.

There is a memory that I keep in my brain - or rather, I try to keep out of my brain - which pops back in there, from time to time. Generally I can go three or four months without ever remembering it, which is a relief. It's one of those things you try and forget about, such is the horror, but which keeps on sneaking back into your mind, whether you want it to or not - and believe me, I want it not; I want not the snot.

But there is no way of keeping it away. Just as my nose leaks with a globby salty tide of mucus, so my brain finds itself overrun with memories it doesn't want, which it seems powerless to keep at bay. And so, no matter how hard I struggle against the inevitable, whenever I have a cold, I remember this.

I am seven years old. It is lunchtime, and I'm at school. We had tables for school dinners and packed lunches. I had packed lunches. I am eating a sandwich cut into quarters - it's probably cheese, or salmon paste, or something inoffensive like that. I don't know why, but my eye is drawn to the boy sitting across the table, to the right, facing me. I am looking at him. And then it happens. It happens every time. I keep wanting it not to happen, but it happens.

From his nostril - his left, my right - comes a dangling worm of snot. Bright green, I promise you. Luminous, almost. The very thought of the colour makes me gag. And I am watching as it pokes its gooey green head out of the nostril and takes a leap with gravity downwards.

This boy - I think his name was Jeremy; he had dandruff and used to get in fights - is unaware of what's happening. And no-one can tell him, because we are all transfixed by the snot-snake tumbling downwards, downwards, so inexorably downwards. He is eating a sandwich. I think it is like my sandwich, cut into quarters, and maybe in wholemeal bread, maybe it's something like an egg sandwich, I don't know. And as he opens his mouth to take a bite, the vast green gusher of snot lands on the sandwich, and before he knows what's going on, he's eaten it.

He's eaten it all! He's eaten his own snot. And he doesn't know it! But I can see it! I can see it all!

At this point, I turn around and retch, and retch, and retch, and retch. I hurl that sandwich onto the wooden bench, as far as my guts can squeeze it.

Even as I type these words, I shudder and retch even now.

I am glad, though, that I have shared that memory with you. If you should ever see me, and I have a cold, and I suddenly get a faraway look in my eyes, and start being sick into a bin, you'll know why. Please forgive me.

Marr's attacks

October 19, 2010

I'm back. I had a great holiday[27]. England is cold and dank and slate-grey and full of grumpy people. I knew I was home when I saw a miserable-looking old lady in a cyan coat at a bus stop with a tartan shopping trolley. And then I read about Andrew Marr[28] saying that bloggers are 'inadequate, pimpled and single' while I was away.

Sigh.

It's tempting, isn't it, to start off by saying "Ooh Andrew Marr, who the hell is *that* fuck-ugly Michael Gove doppelganger to judge others by their physical appearance, the weedy little runt; is he just getting back at others for the repeat bullyings he inevitably endured at school?" - but that would be the lazy blogging of crude stereotype; that would play into his hands and go some way towards

---

[27] I had had a great holiday. This bit was very true indeed.

[28] www.guardian.co.uk/media/2010/oct/11/andrew-marr-bloggers

proving his point. One could even bring up *that thing* about Andrew Marr; but again, that would be wrong too (so don't do it in the comments, please[29]); that would be exactly the kind of nasty blogging that he's obviously read, and didn't like, so why go and confirm his prejudices by playing up to them?

No. And besides, Andrew Marr does have a point. A lot of bloggers *are* inadequate fools, let's not deny that. I'm paraphrasing here, but someone (I think it was Suzanne Moore) said they'd been to a blogging event and it hadn't dispelled the notion of bloggers as sad men masturbating in the spare bedroom. Well, that's kind of what a lot of us are: tragic loners tapping away at a keyboard; losers who blame their own failures and misery on the shortcomings of others, and transform that supposedly righteous anger into swearing and abuse; anonymous cowards who wouldn't squeak at anyone 'in real life' but who develop an online persona that's crusading, powerful and mighty, all the things they in reality lack.

It's a fair cop. And Marr was only having a dig to raise a chortle at some literary event; you can see why someone might be a bit sneery about the online world as opposed to the printed one at such a thing, and maybe he was just

---

[29] Obviously, this being a book rather than a blogpost, you can't comment on it. Well you can slag it off to your heart's content wherever you like, but you can't comment here. It seems rather odd to see a blogpost without comments underneath it; odd but at the same time there's a sense of relief. Anyone who's ever written anything online ever will understand what I mean.

playing to the gallery. I don't think he's sly enough, either, to have made the comments hoping for a wave of disapproval that would have made his point more elegantly than he could ever have done. No, he just said what he said, and that's fair enough. I don't mind at all.

The only thing I would say is that there isn't a taxonomy of bloggers, just as there isn't an easy way to spot a journalist, for example - though you can always have a bash at the latter. (Do they wear corduroy? Do they smell of booze at 8am as if they might have slept in a skip? Do they look a bit shy, and are overcompensating by shouting on the telephone? If they weren't in a newsroom, would they look out of place shuffling around a library all day in soiled, crumpled clothing? Are they driving a *really rubbish car*? Do they look like they got dressed in the dark, and yet somehow seem proud of the fact? And so on...) But just as not all journos are like that, not *all* bloggers are scratchy, marginal characters, 40-year-old virgins or pissant keyboard warriors; some of us actually have lives, and are reasonably ordinary, even pleasant, in real life. No, really.

And Marr is wrong, mind you, to bring up the hoary old 'blogging will never replace journalism' silliness. At the risk of setting up a strawman, since (as someone pointed out to me a while ago) accusing someone of setting up a strawman is becoming something of, er, a strawman, it's a bit of a strawman. I've probably mentioned before I'm doing this thing[30] on Friday, where me and other sad

---

[30] www.watershed.co.uk/exhibits/2535/ - it was a discussion called 'What's the blogging story?' about blogging and

pimpled inadequates will be discussing blogging and journalism and that; can I say now and give fair warning that anyone who says 'blogging will never replace journalism' will get a slap round the face with a dirty, oily old salmon from me? Because that's not the point and it's *never* the point. No-one wants blogging to replace journalism or supersede it; no-one seriously thinks it will, completely, either. Good blogging can and will complement good journalism, while bad blogging, like bad journalism, drags everyone down. And it's healthy to have some of the old guard challenged by new writers - they'll either up their game or get washed away with the tide. Competition is good for all of us, rubbish amateurs like me and established silky craftsmen like Marr.

So while it's tempting to stick two fingers up to someone like Marr, he's a mainly harmless cove really. He's got a bit of a point, as well. Though it's not true of all of us. I think. Hope. Something.[31]

---

bloggers. Marr's quote was brought up. I was quite awkward and didn't really say much. That is comforting, in a way.

[31] I'm not always very good at ending blogposts, but on this occasion I will attempt to say that it was a kind of deliberate bathos. I am showing my ineptitude as a blogger/writer by failing to come to a firm conclusion, flattering Andrew Marr and almost making his version of events seem more likely than mine. I have gone through a whole article about Marr without using the word 'goblinlike', so I think it's fair to assume I am trying to do something a little different here.

Why I don't want Thatcher to die[32]

October 21, 2010

It's funny, but the feeling that's crept across me over the past few days, upon hearing that Margaret Thatcher is ill and might not make it, is not one of joy. I thought it would be, but it isn't. No, the overwhelming feeling is something approaching disappointment, and sadness.

Sure, if you'd asked me a week or so ago whether I'd be happy at the imminent death of someone whose entire worldview and actions I find despicable, I'd have said yes. I'd have said more than yes; I'd have been dancing through the streets in a giant sombrero, shooting fireworks into the night sky, singing Ding Dong The Witch Is Dead. I'd have been delighted at the thought of Thatcher finally getting in a grave so we could all piss on it.

Not now.

---

[32] Margaret Thatcher had been treated in hospital and there were whispers that she wouldn't pull through. Happily, these turned out not to be true and she recovered.

Maybe I'm getting more mature in my 30s than I was when I was younger. Maybe I don't find the idea of an elderly lady snuffing it all that appealing. But I don't think that it's that, either. I still do wish ill and death upon people that I don't like, and I don't see anything tremendously wrong with that, and I don't think that's going to change. I've wished her, and others, ill in the past, and I don't really regret it, though that nastiness seems to be going away a little, the older I get, the closer I get to snuffing it myself, the nearer me and my friends and family get to an appointment with a furnace.

But there's more to it than that.

The reason why I feel sad is that I want Margaret Thatcher to live a long and healthy life - and I think all self-respecting lefties should, as well. And I'll tell you why. I want her to live, to see a day when the things she believes in are not just discredited, and despised, but overturned, and consigned to the wreckage of history.

I want her to live, to see a day when she is rightly regarded as a poisonous and terrible influence on Britain and the world - not just by the usual suspects, or by those who suffered at her hands and those of her friends Botha, Reagan and Pinochet, but by the vast majority of people.

I want her to live a long and full and healthy life where she can see that the things she did were truly disastrous - and, while, I don't wish ill upon the country and I hope that I'm wrong about the effect of her heirs' cuts on the country, I want her to live to see the day that her brand of me-first neoliberalism is shown to be a horrific stain upon the world, and not a solution to anything at all.

You might say I'm naive. I'm used to being called that. But I do think that, regardless of what I think of the vile woman, she believed she was doing the right thing. You might argue against that, and I don't mind, but if I'm right, and she did, and she could live long enough to be shown that everything she believed in was wrong, that would be better than her dying now, frail and old, in a hospital somewhere, to the ringing endorsements of right-wingers everywhere.

If she dies now, it's perfect timing, in a way. You can see David Cameron carrying on the torch from her at her deathbed. The cry of "Let's do it for Maggie!" will go up. The obituaries will be glowing towards the 'Iron Lady' and her legacy - I have a feeling they always will be, I'm afraid - in the newspapers who eagerly enjoyed her policies then, and who eagerly enjoy her successors' policies today.

No. I don't want her to die and I don't want her to suffer. I want her to live. I want her to live to see the day when she's proved wrong. I want her to suffer remorse and regret for the things she has done, not slip away from this life feeling free, with a sense of righteousness and vindication. I know that's probably a stupid thought, and one which is ridiculously doomed, but I don't care. I don't want her to suffer, and I don't want her to die. Not until the day she's shown to be wrong and acknowledged to be wrong by the vast majority of people.

And then she can go to hell.

Scepticism, woo, magic, weirdness and tinfoil hats

January 6, 2011

This book review by Ben Six[33] is a lovely thing and I recommend you take some time to have a look at it, because it really got me thinking. It's very pleasantly written as well:

One can only hope that such admissions point the way to fruitful comradeship. Not that I'm demanding limp accomodationism – "You believe in telepathy? Well, I always know when my wife's in a mood!" – it just seems like collaboration might bust the unfortunate perception that sensible sceptics are forever batting down the potty paranormalists. McLuhan, never rude but prone – who isn't? – to the odd generalisation seems impatient with the more obdurate critics. At one point he sighs that – like, perhaps, the spoilt teenage girls in U.S. reality shows: huffing that their limousines aren't the desired shade of pink – they'd nitpick with any experiment, however rigorous. Even if that's true the goal should surely be to make one's tests so thorough that complaints would sound implausible to the agnostics. And, hey, one might as well retain some trust in the good faith of others. Remembering the one-time doubters of the early psychics,

---

[33] bensix.wordpress.com/2011/01/03/consciousnessess-maimed-randis-prize-and-the-challenge-of-the-paranormal/

researchers in speculative fields should be wary of polarizing believers and their critics.

Now I consider myself as a sceptic, an atheist, a lover of science, and all of that, and quite pleased (if not smug, hopefully) about it all. But I think what BenSix uncovers through his review of *Randi's Prize* is something that I've been feeling in my water for a while (yes yes, I *know*, that's kind of the point) about the related ideas of scepticism and atheism - I find that, although I by and large subscribe to those schools of thought, there's something faintly unsatisfying about them. I find it faintly unsatisfying, anyway; for others, it may be perfectly fine. But let me try and explain.

Firstly, I don't have a problem with religion nowadays. I used to be a lot more of a shrill atheist than I am nowadays, for which I inevitably offer the meek and slightly hot-faced shameful apology of a bleeding heart. But now, I don't know. I think it is a really important part of people's lives - and I don't mean that in a supercilious "Oh, this must fulfil some kind of cultural/biological need and I'm sure it's a comfort for you" way, but in the sense of feeling that I really envy the joy, peace and happiness that people do get from their faiths and beliefs.

I can't share it because I don't really believe in any god or gods, and that's that; and I don't consider myself less of a good person, or less of a spiritually nourished person, because of my lack of faith or belief; it's just that I think a lot of people do find a good way of that enrichment through the things they sincerely do feel and believe, and who am I to question that? I have to choose a different path personally; not a wrong one, or a less good one, just a different one.

And I'm aware that religion has caused countless deaths, and misery; but faith, perhaps, has not caused so many - the personal faith, the kind of prayer and belief that Jesus Christ spoke about in the sermon on the mount, which is still a text that resonates with me, despite the fact I don't really believe the man ever existed, or was the son of god, or any of that. That doesn't matter: the idea of a personal spiritual relationship with the world is something that can be benign, and helpful, and a force for good.

Secondly, I have come to look at the term 'woo' as something a little snippy, kind of ugly, if that's the right word. You know, the "Oh, you believe in something that's not scientifically proven, you listen to anecdotes rather than peer-reviewed science; that's woo." Well, it may very well be, but I like the idea of being curious rather than shutting things off. I think curiosity is such a valuable part of science and exploration; without curiosity, we wouldn't have the scientific near-certainties we enjoy today. I don't like dismissing anything that doesn't fall neatly into certain parameters as 'woo'; it's a bit confrontational, aggressive maybe. Woo is the sceptical community's blasphemy if you like, and is occasionally pursued with similar zeal. Yes yes, oh the irony, but I don't care about that side of it; I'm more interested in a missed opportunity.

Which isn't to say there aren't charlatans out there, because there are; and it isn't to say that people exploit other people by making false claims, because they do; and it's not to say that people shouldn't be sceptical of claims that aren't proven, because they should. But it's something a little different from all of that. When you look at something like the recent mass deaths of birds, it provokes in me a huge curiosity. How the hell did this happen?

How did it all go on? What does this even mean? Is it evidence of something or evidence of nothing?

It's not a short bus ride from there, unfortunately in my view, to the people who will tell you, with a serious and solemn face, that this represents the exposure of a secret weapon, that there is murder and intrigue involved, that this proves that contrails are spraying us with chemicals, and all of that. Can't we find a middle way between the tinfoil hat - to use another pejorative term for folks who take a different view of stuff - and the cold scientific rationalisation? If there is uncertainty and a mystery that can't easily be explained, I find something to enjoy about all that, and rejoice in. With stories like that, curiosity is what draws people in; people like a mystery and something that isn't easily solved, and patting them on the head and telling them we know what it is, even when we don't, most likely frustrates them, I think.

I love complexity and I think that's part of scepticism, if indeed scepticism a type of thought or a way of thinking at all, and I'm not always entirely sure it is. I love the idea that things aren't as simple as they're presented, and that there's always another layer underneath, if you keep digging - it's why I like chipping away at tabloid narratives all the time, to see what's really underneath and whether the presentation of facts stacks up against the available evidence.

I say this because there are, in my experience, things which have puzzled me and confused me and stung my curiosity, and for which I have no explanation. Many people, perhaps, experience similar things, but tell themselves not to be so stupid. And I have no idea as to why these things could have happened, or what they represent, or anything. But all I do know is this: I have known a couple of people, very near to death, who have experienced extremely vivid meetings with their parents, or ancestors, or dead friends.

You can rationalise it, if you like, and imagine that's the human brain comforting itself somehow at the point of death; but I fail to see the advantage, evolutionary or otherwise, in that kind of phenomenon. And I have heard this kind of thing from others - experiencing intimate contact with people who have recently died, as if they were still present; or having a sense that someone would die on a particular day; or when close relatives, even when separated from each other, die at the same time; or, more importantly, the testimony of those who are about to die, and what they say they are seeing and feeling. There's a certain amount you can put down to palliative care, or drugs of one kind or another, and whatever, but is it just that 'sceptics' sometimes force themselves to look for rational explanations, just as 'woo' types force themselves to look at spiritual ones?

I don't know what it means or what happened or why, because I have not experienced it myself - I'm still very much alive. You can say it's some kind of cultural projection, some kind of meeting of expectations, something like that, and maybe it is, and I'm not ruling that out; but I am curious. I have a curiosity as to whether that is what it is - and I speak as someone who thinks that when you die, that's that. That's what I believe, but I have these strange events which point in the other direction.

That's the complexity to enjoy.

That's the kind of complexity that just makes you wonder,

and want to know more, and to delve into the science, and the anecdotes. Sure, there are a lot of anecdotes involved with these things, but then that is because we have eyes and ears and brains to process it all with; why have those ways of experiencing the world if you won't trust what they tell you? I find it hard to trust a book rather than what I have seen and heard, and that is why, I imagine, so do other people.

It's that curiosity that keeps burning, and which I don't want to see go anywhere. It's also the reason that, even though I don't believe in life after death or religion of any kind, I try to keep what you might call an open mind. Not in the hope or expectation of ever having the curiosity satisfied, but just because it feels the right thing to do. And despite what I might think about 'woo' or magic or weirdness of any kind, why I refuse to close these things off forever.

This is a blogpost about Stephen Fry[34]

---

[34] Stephen Fry got into trouble for an interview with a gay magazine in which he had made a jokey comparison between male gay sexuality and female straight sexuality. A lot of people didn't see the funny side, and there followed a slew of articles to try and capitalise on the Twitter-friendly Fry connection. This was my attempt to do a meta-article before those ones hit the web, to point out what was going on. I

October 31, 2010

This is a blogpost about Stephen Fry. Ooh, isn't it? Stephen Fry something or other did something. Twitterstorm, isn't it? Grumble grumble misogyny or something or nothing. Flouncing? Yes. On the receiving end for once. More than a million followers. Claims he's been misquoted, but, isn't it? Counterintuitive: is there really anything wrong with what he said? Countercounterintuitive: Yes, there was certainly something wrong, even though it might seem counterintuitive to ask if there's really anything wrong with what he said? Hmm, yes. Gay men talking about women? What would they know anyway? Or perhaps they would know, maybe? Don't rule that out. Jan Moir or something,[35] yes. Self-styled Twitter guru now the Antichrist. Some examples of other celebrities on Twitter getting annoyed with stuff. Just the latest in a long line. Does it mark the end of the Twitter honeymoon for celebrities? Does it mark the end of Twitter in itself? Has the Twitter mob gone berserk, or is this just righteous indignation? I have no answers, just rambling prose.

---

think it worked, and Fry eventually returned to Twitter after a gentle flounce, so all was well in the end.

[35] As I predicted, quite a few grumpy writers did make this association between Fry's displeasure over Jan Moir's appalling article, and his own somewhat less offensive words. Because there's a whole army of people out there just waiting to try and find a grain of hypocrisy and shout "Aha!" – maybe I've been one of them, but I find myself doing it less and less. I find it quite annoying.

Counterintuitive: Fry's outburst and the subsequent storm proves that the mob he helped create has now turned on its idols.

Countercounterintuitive: Fry's outburst is quite understandable really. Personal: I'm a woman and I love sex, Stephen Fry! Impersonal: I'm not a woman, but I love sex, Stephen Fry! Personal: I'm a gay man and I don't love sex, I love relationships, Stephen Fry! Impersonal: I'm not a woman, or a gay man, so I don't really know anything about any of this, but I'll harumph anyway. Yes. Stephen Fry or something, or nothing. The latest in a long line of Twitterstorms, ironically something about the irony of the situation.

Will this do?[36]

I've finally worked out why I don't like the X-Factor

November 8, 2010

I know, it's hardly controversial or counterintuitive to think that the X-Factor is bad. But something has been

---

[36] On reflection I really ought to have submitted this to Comment is Free. I think it might've been a goer.

nagging away at me for a while. I find bits of the X-Factor all right - watchable, even - but others make me want to pour bleach in my eyes and whack my teeth out with a toffee hammer while rocking back and forth. Why should that be?

I think I've finally worked it out, though, and I present them here in list form.

Louis Walsh shouting over whooping and applause. I hate this. I hate this more than anything, ever. CHER! CHER! CHER! CHER! CHER! CHER, YOU'RE ONE OF THE MOST AMAZING... CHER... YOU'RE ONE OF THE MOST AMAZING... CHER... Shut up! Shut up! Wait for them to finish, or someone tell them to be quiet, or something.

Simon Cowell's wink. What's he winking for? Some kind of shared joke between him and us? Is it something like "These teeth cost more than your fucking car, and I know it, and you know it, and yet for some unfathomable reason, I'm popular and you're a nobody"? Is it that?

Cheryl Cole's 'serious/thinking' face. Hmm, I am thinking about what I am hearing... hmm, I am serious and thinking about this. Hmm. Yes, I am not just a pop star, I am a role model for CONFIDENT WOMEN EVERYWHERE. Hmm... I am listening to this song and thinking about my comments afterwards, yes... and I might sort of get a bit choked up about it or something... yes. What Joey from Friends would call "Smell the fart acting".

The fact that I'm meant to know whose these bloody

people are. That their faces are splashed over all those horrible garish dentist's waiting room magazines all week. Ooh, Katie did something. Ooh, Cher did something. Ooh, the creepy-faced one who looks like a boring Perez Hilton did something. I daresay they all bloody did something. I imagine they went to the toilet, and had lunch somewhere, and did lots of other stuff. What is this bloody need for a backstory and a soap opera?

They can't, when all is said and done, sing very well. Yet I get told afterwards, by people who apparently know these things, that their vocals were 'amazing' and 'incredible'. No they weren't, I've got ears, I can tell. They're mediocre singers doing something reasonably well - you can admire the composure under pressure, the sudden rise to fame and all that, but amazing? Incredible?

What in the wide world of sports is this choreography? People on bicycles? Fire? People on fire on bicycles? What kind of madness is this?

The fake enmity between the judges. Oh for fuck's sake. Cowell and Walsh have worked together for about 20 years and made each other incredibly rich men. They have the same, appalling, taste in middle-of-the-road banal shit that makes Michael Buble look edgy, yet we're supposed to believe they're always at each other's throats. Piss off. Ooh and Dannii and Cheryl are having some kind of 'style war' or whatever behind the scenes. Toss.

That, despite knowing all of this, I get sucked into the bloody programme. Why can't I just leave it alone? Why can't I just not watch it? Is it because everyone else watches it and I reason that there must be something quite good about it, if they all enjoy it? Is it because it's a guilty pleasure? Is it because there's nothing any good on the other side?

Race and racism: A white Briton writes

November 18, 2010

When I fill in those diversity forms for job applications, I always put 'White British' or 'White English', or whatever variant I'm meant to use. That's what I am, although it seems so clumsy: what is 'white British' anyway and who gets to be that rather than, say, mixed race British? How mixed does your race have to be before you're mixed race?

And how white is white? I have no idea. Does my gypsy grandmother count as 'white', or should that lineage be viewed as 'mixed race'? I don't know. I am usually pink, and I was born in Britain, so there you have it: white British. Should I be proud of that, scared of it, worried about the fact that people like me are being apparently overwhelmed, or just ambivalent about the whole thing? I don't know. I think you're much less aware of your ethnicity and your heritage if you're in the majority; you grow up knowing that most people are like you, no matter how you mix at school, or work, or whatever.

Being 'white British', if I must call myself that, though, gives me an insight into the kind of articles that we've seen splashed over the newspapers today - and may see more of tomorrow - about how 'white Britons', people like me, might - that's might, not will - no longer be in the majority by the time I'm 91 years old.

I don't know if I'll really care, if I make it to 91, whether there are more slightly darker faces than mine walking around; or whether I'll care very much if there are more pink faces belonging to people who didn't grow up in Britain, either. Maybe that's just me, but I don't see what the big fuss is about. I really don't, and I can say this as a 'white Briton': I don't care.

People say it's a taboo to talk about immigration, but of course that's not the case. I say it's a taboo to talk positively of immigration, as if it's something that isn't a great deluge to be feared. And 'white' does not equal 'British'; 'British' does not equal 'white'. If white Britons *do* get 'outnumbered', that might not be a tremendously bad thing. These islands do not belong to whites, the same way that they don't belong to anyone. White people happen to have lived here since the Ice Age, but a lot of things have changed since then.

Human beings are migratory animals in a lot of ways, and now we have aircraft and all sorts of technological advances to speed up that process; you can't see a nation state as being composed of a particular ethnic group. Increasingly, it doesn't work that way. Britain is more of a cultural than a racial identity, I think, and that identity is more multicultural the more immigration we have - and do you know what, I don't think that's a bad thing at all.

These articles do, as ever, come with the same old agenda

- the agenda that there are 'Brits' and there are others - it's the them and us thing all over again. I don't see it that way; I see it as us and us. So there are other races than white coming over to this country and living here? Good for them. So it might mean that white people - the 'indigenous population' so beloved of dog-whistle racists everywhere - are not in the absolute overall majority in fifty or so years' time? Well, so what. This is where I struggle to find a problem, where I struggle to find the fear.

One of the reasons why I do love living in this country - and I do, by the way - is the way in which it is such a cosmopolitan place. 'Our' history and heritage is not under threat. 'Our' country is not being taken over. There'll still be a place for the cricket on village greens and warm pints of beer of John Major's wistful vision; but maybe the country is changing in more ways than just the shades of the faces of the people who live here, and maybe there are more things to be concerned about than that.

What makes me angry is when it's assumed that 'white Britons' like me are automatically opposed to all kinds of change; that somehow I should go along with this panic porn about immigration because somehow it's me who is under threat. Well that's simply not true. I'm not under threat. I'm intensely relaxed about it all. If I do make it to 91, and if I am no longer as a pink-skinned person in the majority, I won't be shedding too many tears. I dare say if I ever have children they may have children with 'non-white' partners, or maybe they won't; but if they do, I'll be happy. I'm not scared by the scaremongering. My race isn't under threat. So I refuse to go along with any of this. Those who worry about the apparent decline of the 'white

Briton' don't speak for this white Briton. You don't speak for me.[37]

Let's burn things*

November 12, 2010

Let's burn things. Want to get on the front page of a newspaper, but know that no-one's going to listen to you otherwise? Burn things. They love it. They're like moths; they can't help flapping towards a flame. If it's on fire, it's good. Want to do a decent protest with reasonable aims? Forget it. Page 206. Smash something, though - or, even better, burn it - and you'll be flying towards the front of the paper. Burn something.[38] Burn it because you want to

---

[37] I received a few delightful responses to this article, calling me a cunt and a traitor to the white race. Which is always disappointing, and makes you feel a bit gloomy for a while, because you remember that there are people out there, beyond trolling, beyond just shouting on the internet, who really believe that stuff. I hope they're becoming a minority, but I have no way of knowing; I just like to be optimistic and think those kind of views are becoming more marginalised. All the same, it's not nice to be confronted with them in abusive emails and comments.

[38] This post came at a time when student protests were only getting coverage if stuff got burnt. If my heavy-handed

get attention. And it'll work. If you're the leader of a tiny load of idiots whose entire membership would fit in a Ford Cortina, yet you want to get massive attention way out of proportion to (a) whether anyone should actually give a shit about you or not and (b) the value of your needle-dicked protest in the bigger scheme of things, then don't worry - burn things. Burn something that people see as a symbol of something noble; that'll do the trick. Kerching! Your poxy one-man-and-his-dog protest will be transformed from some nutcase ranting away in the middle of nowhere into LOOK AT ALL OF THEM, YES THOSE DARK ONES, THEY'RE BURNING STUFF AND HATE US AND ALL THE VALUES WE HOLD DEAR, THEY HATE OUR BRAVE BOYS, LET'S KICK THEM OUT, OH THEY'RE FROM HERE ANYWAY, THAT JUST MAKES ME ANGRY AND SOMEWHAT FRUSTRATED. Burn stuff, and hey presto - your insignificant piddly little life gets transformed from the no-mark you so richly deserve to be into a big scary bogeyman coming to kill the middle classes. Brilliant! Just what you always wanted. Burn stuff. Burn it high and burn it long. Though make sure there's a crescent of cameras around you to capture the full richness of what you're doing in glorious colour, otherwise there's no point. Burn things. Burn them because you like to watch them burn. Burn them because that's how it's decided whether things are important or not - on fire good, not on fire bad. Because that's the way we love it.

* The title of this post is not to be taken as an incitement

---

sledgehammer delivery hadn't made that completely fucking obvious.

to burn things, especially not airports, or public buildings, or Conservative Party headquarters, or nice shops that sell charity Christmas cards, or anywhere really, please don't arrest me, don't send me back to that scary place...[39]

The 'squeezed middle' and class conflict

November 28, 2010

I suppose I am one of those many millions of people who might get lumped in with Ed Miliband's 'Squeezed Middle'.[40] I've got a slightly below average income, I have a mortgage, I pay my taxes - whether I'm the '*hardworking* taxpayer' or not isn't really my call to make, but I go to work every day - I stick diesel into my car once a week, and I buy stuff. I am one of The Squeezed Middle.

---

[39] This is a reference to the Twitter joke trial of Paul Chambers, which was going on at the time, where a man had been convicted of threatening behaviour due to a jokey tweet about blowing up Robin Hood Airport. Consequently I was overplaying the whole 'this isn't an incitement to do anything nasty' line.

[40] www.bbc.co.uk/news/uk-politics-11848303 The newly elected Labour leader had decided to worry about the 'squeezed middle' first.

The hardworking taxpayer. You know, a moron.

As I said the other day when discussing Howard Flight's depressingly nasty swipe at the poor[41], there's something artificial about the whole 'class war' business, regardless of who's doing the fighting. It suits our leaders to blame the poor for the fact that the middle classes and the rich have to pay taxes, but it's not quite the whole picture. *If only these lazy so-and-sos got off their poor working-class arses and contributed their taxes, then we wouldn't have to spend so much out of our wage packets... if only so many horrible Europeans didn't come over here and steal jobs from Brits who could do them, then more people could work, and we wouldn't be paying so much...* but it's a great deal more complicated than that. However, it suits a government of whatever colour to point the finger at those on benefits, and immigrants, and walk off whistling. While we're doing all the fighting, they're counting the spoils.

But here I am, one of the 'Squeezed Middle' (tm), having to see a large lump of money deducted from my wages before I even see it, and there it goes, to pay for hospitals, and schools, and roads, and poor people... I must be *livid*, mustn't I? Except... well, no. It would be wrong, of course, to say I've never had it so good; the threat of redundancy looms in my profession, as in many others,

---

[41] enemiesofreason.co.uk/2010/11/25/breeding-hell/ - Tory peer Howard Flight had said: "We're going to have a system where the middle classes are discouraged from breeding because it's jolly expensive. But for those on benefits, there is every incentive."

though I'm certainly not in as much peril as a lot of public sector workers. And yes, in my particular case, three years of not having a pay rise isn't spectacularly fun, when inflation has been there, doing its worst. Sure, the mortgage has come down a bit, but not an enormous amount.

But... things are not terrible. I have a job. I have a job, and I am very grateful for that. I might not have a wonderful job, and I may not find it the most fulfilling thing in the world, but so what? It's a job. I get to pay for things. I get to go on holidays, and go out every now and then. Having been unemployed in the past - though not for a long time - I remember the feeling of awfulness it brings, the feeling of pain. Call me a bleeding-heart left-liberal bastard if you like - I see it as a badge of honour - but I don't think most people who are without a job are jollying it up and having a whale of a time in a world of daytime telly and Tesco Value. Things might be a bit tougher for me than they were two or three years ago, but it could be a lot worse.

Tell you what I don't do though. I don't ring up radio phone-ins going "Cor, these bladdy public sector workers don't bladdy know they're born, they should all be sacked, I've not had a bleedin pay rise for three bleedin years!" because that would make me (a) the kind of tosser who phones up FiveLive or TalkSport in the first place, and (b) the kind of malicious toerag who wishes harm upon all others just because I've been having a bit of a rough trot. Sure, things might have not been spectacular for my personal circumstances recently, but I don't want everyone else to have it the same, or worse. If other people have better pay and conditions, good for them; that's what everyone should have. I don't want the public sector dragged down to the level of the worst private sector companies, just because that'll show them; that kind of attitude is deeply unpleasant, and makes it worse for everyone.

The Squeezed Middle? Spare me. Things are certainly a bit tougher for a lot of us, but I'd still rather be here, in a job and paying tax, than being out of work. Because that is where the struggle really is; that is where the pain is really being felt. We might feel we have it bad, having to cut back on this, that or the other, but I'd rather not swap with someone on Jobseekers. That's how good it is to have a job - no matter how much it gets irritating, annoying or upsetting to have one, it's still a hundred times better than not having one. The Squeezed Middle is still a much, much better place to be than the bottom. Trouble is, the Squeezed Middle is going to get smaller, and those even worse off than that are going to grow in number. That's where the real problems are coming.

Would a little 'War on Christmas' be a terrible thing?[42]

---

[42] This is a kind of misleading headline, which I suppose I did deliberately to try and bring some readers in. Even so, I imagine it leaves me open to the kind of criticism I have often given tabloids for using misleading headlines. But at the time I was trying to play around with people's expectations of what I was going to produce with the blog.

November 29, 2010

I wrote on Saturday about Eric Pickles's pandering to tabloid mythology[43] when it came to the 'War on Christmas'. Many of my fellow media bloggers have written about just how wrong Pickles is; Primly Stable[44] has written to Eric Pickles very politely correcting him on his wrongness, for example.

But it got me thinking: if there really were a little War on Christmas, would it be such a bad thing?

I don't mean literally a war on Christmas. That would be bad. Well, if you could literally have a War on Christmas, which I doubt you could. But still. Anything which meant that Christians couldn't celebrate Christmas, or were afraid to rejoice in the appearance of the little be-haloed babber in the cow shed, would be terrible. No, I mean, what if the so-called politically correct brigade dared to let us all recognise that Christmas wasn't *just* about Him, and was *also* about other stuff. Would that be so wrong?

I speak as someone who proudly appeared as the Virgin Mary in my primary school nativity play (it was an all boys' school, all right?) and who uttered the immortal words: "I

---

43 enemiesofreason.co.uk/2010/11/27/merry-christmas-eric-pickles-you-dimwit/ - Eric Pickles had written about Christianity being at risk of being 'marginalised'.

44 primlystable.blogspot.com/2010/11/letter-to-eric-pickles.html

will do the Lord's bidding" before nearly dropping the infant Jesus into the front row of dewy-eyed parents. There's nothing wrong with nativity plays - very nice story, and all that - or nativity scenes, or going to church, or singing Christmas carols, or using the word 'Christmas' rather than 'Yuletide' or anything like that. Nothing wrong with any of it, and I know it's a wonderful celebration for an awful lot of people. That's great, and no-one's trying to take that away from anyone.

But... that isn't everything about this time of year and the traditional celebrations. It isn't solely about the birth of Jesus of Nazareth - there are a whole lot of other winter traditions that take place at exactly the same time as Christmas, ancient stuff and modern stuff too; and besides, the birth of Christ probably didn't take place on December 25, if it happened at all. It seems a bit silly for people to demand that we celebrate the birth of Jesus, and only the birth of Jesus, at this time of year; it smacks, a bit, of flexing our cultural muscles to slap down minorities and demand they do the same as us.

Just as our Springfest Easter eggs have been appropriated by Christianity as 'symbols of the tomb', so a lot of our other pagan Winterfest gubbins has been scooped up too - the 'Christmas' tree and the Yule log, for example. Just as it's not wrong to think of Xmas* as being a little boy in a manger, it's not wrong to think of it as Papa Noel, or Father Christmas (not Saint Nicholas!), or tinsel, or snowmen, or Wizzard, or Christmas trees, or snowflakes, or cheerful robins on cards, or In The Bleak Midwinter, Frosty Wind Made Moan, or It's A Wonderful Life, or Shirley Bassey sticking her foot through the floor in the Morecambe and Wise Christmas special, or decorations, or turkey, or sausages wrapped in bacon, or plum duff, or crackers, or The Two Ronnies, or any, or all, of that jazz.

Why not? We all see Christmas in different ways. For a lot of us it isn't necessarily a devoted religious festival, which doesn't mean we don't respect the rights of those who do see it that way; it just means there's room for both. It's as much Noddy Holder on the radio and Only Fools and Horses on the TV as it is turning up for Midnight Mass; it's as much giving presents and being slightly disappointed with terrible socks as it is devoting a day to remembering the birth of our Lord.

I think there's room for lots of religious fun and lots of fun for everyone else as well. I don't want to be a po-faced atheist sitting like Scrooge and saying Bah Humbug to it all; I love the idea of lots of Christians having fun in their celebrations, and besides, I want some bloody presents and an excuse to cane a bottle of ruby port, all right? But I think it's not fair, either, for anyone to think that if you don't celebrate Christmas religiously, you're not celebrating it properly. No-one's banning Christmas. Being inclusive to other faiths doesn't mean you're being somehow disrespectful to the beardy guy with the holes in his hands; it just means you're thinking of others, which I'd say is quite a Christian attitude.

Anyway, there you go. Crack out the eggnog and the mince pies, and let us make merry. December is nearly upon us and I'm about to raid the advent calendar. Can we just forget about the 'war on Christmas' this year, and have a festive Winterfest truce? Here's hoping...

* Also: there's nothing wrong with Xmas. The X stands for the Greek letter Chi, meaning Christ, so it's just a

bloody abbreviation already. It's not 'taking the Christ out of Christmas' as a billion green-ink letter writers will have you believe.

What they say and what they mean

December 13, 2010

A little guide by me into what some people (on the internet and elsewhere) say and what they actually mean.

"So let me get this right" - Let me deliberately get this wrong, reducing all arguments to absurd oversimplification.

"Just saying" - I'm not 'just saying'; but if you take offence at this barbed comment, I will act all surprised and horrified. I am, after all, just saying!

"No offence" - I mean quite a considerable amount of offence.

"I'm not racist..." - I am racist.

"Don't take this the wrong way" - as anything other than an insult.

"But will you also condemn XX atrocity by YY?" -

look, the brown bastards are WORSE than whitey.

"You wouldn't be as keen to criticise Muslims, would you?" - look, the brown bastards are WORSE than whitey.

"Funny you didn't mention incident ZZ which also happened recently..." - look, the brown bastards are WORSE than whitey.

"A deafening silence from you on that one" - because you fail to mention something irrelevant and obscure, this means you are a hypocrite.

"I thought you were meant to be a liberal" - I hate liberals, but if liberals don't react in a way in which I assume liberals, whom I hate, should react, I can say they're hypocrites.

"So much for freedom of speech!" - Since you refused to print my pointless inflammatory racist comment, you are the bad guy.

"Of course, you can't say it nowadays" - because some people think racism is a bad thing, or something, it's become disgracefully socially unacceptable to just go around being a racist.

"At last, someone brave enough to tell the truth" - at last, a bigot saying something bigoted in public.

"If you took off your PC rose-tinted glasses for a minute" - and popped on my jaundice-tinted bigoted ones, you'd see things as I do.

"Nice post, but what about XXX?" - what about something entirely unrelated, which I can try and engage you with in abysmal circular discussion for about 55 years?

"This post is biased" - and so am I, but my bias is the nice, allowed kind, while yours is the evil, bad sort.

"This blog post isn't objective" - unlike my trolling comment underneath, obviously; and yes, I have wilfully misunderstood the idea of a lot of blog posts[45].

Lefty-baiting: an idiot's guide

December 17, 2010

Lefty-baiting is a hilarious fun game for all the family - we all know that. But what are the rules, and how do you do it? Here's a simple step-by-step guide to getting it done - right first time, every time. Your Cohens, your Burchills, your Littlejohns, even your Moirs - they know how it's done. If you want to have a go at a lefty but aren't quite

---

[45] I forgot to include "TL:DR" (too long: didn't read), which translates roughly as "I should be very grateful if someone could end my miserable existence in whatever brutal fashion seems most appropriate".

sure where to begin, then worry no longer. That smug comment you want to write at Harry's Place will soon be flowing from your fingertips. You'll be using the word 'hypocrite' as if it's second nature.

1. The Left. Yes, the Left. Capital L preferred. That means everyone from Castro to Polly Toynbee to Tony Blair. Everyone. All of them. They're all doing the same thing, because, well, they all think the same way. This is a useful way of getting things started. If you want to have a crack at Robert Fisk but don't know where to start, why not criticise him for something Gordon Brown did? They're both The Left, so therefore one is responsible for everything the other does.

2. The Left is doing X because of their so-called liberal values. This has a twofold purpose: you get to be supercilious *and* knock up a cheeky strawman in the meantime. Oh look at them with their so-called liberal values; I daresay they do think they're doing the right thing, but of course they're misguided because they're not as clever as me! Now that you've established the apparent motivation for X, regardless of what is actually motivating it, you can show later on that this is actually inconsistent and therefore worthy of the 'hypocrite' label.

Let's use an example to illustrate this. Say someone on the Left - it could be Johann Hari or Kim-Jong Il, they're pretty much interchangeable for our purposes - has said that it's not a terrifically good thing for people to be prejudiced against Muslims. At this point you can roll your eyes and say "Well, I suppose they would think they're doing the right thing, what with their misguided sense of soi-disant liberalism..." before you move in for the kill.

3. The Left is doing X because of their so-called liberal values, but they're actually being the very thing they're complaining about! Nearly there now. You're almost ready to get furiously typing in that box on the Comment is Free website, but let me walk you through this bit first. Remember when we talked about the Left's motivation for doing whatever it is they're doing? Now that you've established that strawman, you need to use it against them by showing them to be just as incorrect as they're accusing others of being.

Remember our example about so-called liberals wanting to be so-called tolerant of so-called Muslims - here you would say "Oh, I suppose these liberals are happy for our Muslim friends to hate homosexuals and stone women to death? That doesn't seem very tolerant towards women!" - what you've done there is perfect. First, you've linked all of Islam with extremism; second, you've accused lefties of being intolerant through their very tolerance. Job done? Well, not quite...

4. The Left is doing X because of their so-called liberal values, but they're actually being the very thing they're complaining about! The hypocrites. It's vitally important to get the H-word out. You need to spray it (ahem) liberally around your column / blog comment to point out (a) the horribleness of the Left in being so stupid they can't understand why they're being hypocrites and (b) the horribleness of the Left in saying some people are 'more equal than others' in their desperation to be politically correct.

Congratulations! You're now ready to get that boilerplate lefty-baiting attack done. Once you're feeling comfortable repeating the same tedious arguments again and again and again and again, never listening to anything anyone else ever says, you can move on to advanced lefty-baiting. Here are some themes you might want to develop once you've seemingly exhausted every option:

"I was a bit of a lefty once, everyone supported the IRA and wanted to boil Jews alive, that's why I stopped being one."[46]

"What the Left appear to want is to capitulate to Osama Bin Laden..."

"Of course, they talk a lot about freedom, but they're the first who want to shut down debate (by which I mean lying racism)..."

Have fun! And remember: try not to think too much. It'll only hurt!

Two-minute hate

December 22, 2010

THIS IS AN ADVERTISEMENT. CONTENT OF THIS BLOGPOST WILL START IN TWO MINUTES. AFTER YOU'VE SAT THROUGH SOME SHIT ABOUT A FUCKING LAND ROVER OR

---

46 I think I'd been reading Julie Burchill at the time.

SOMETHING. OH DON'T YOU TRY AND CLICK THE X. OH NO, MATEY. YOU TRY AND DO THAT AND WE'LL JUST STAMP OUR FEET AND MAKE YOU HAVE TO START AGAIN. FROM THE BEGINNING. YOU JUST SIT THERE AND WAIT. SIT THROUGH ALL OF THIS FUCKING ADVERT. FEEL IT BURN INTO YOUR EYES. TWO WHOLE MINUTES OF YOUR LIFE TICKING BY. TICK, TICK, TICK. THINK OF ALL THE THINGS YOU COULD BE DOING INSTEAD OF WAITING FOR THIS ADVERT TO FINISH. MAKING A BOILED EGG. HAVING A CUP OF TEA. STARING OUT OF THE WINDOW. ANYTHING, REALLY, EXCEPT FOR THIS. BUY A LAND ROVER. USE THESE INSURERS. DO THIS SHIT. IT'S LIKE HAVING A TELEVISION BUT WORSE, SO MUCH WORSE. YOU CHOSE TO CLICK ON THIS. THE THING YOU WANT TO SEE WILL HAPPEN IN TWO MINUTES' TIME AND THERE'S NO WAY AROUND IT.

Yes yes, I'd like to see that video, you know the one. Yes, that video. It looked good, like it might be fun or something, and, oh, that's it is it. Jesus. Two minutes of advert for ten fucking seconds of a cat falling over? Fuck me. Is this what my life has come to?

OH SO YOU'VE CLICKED ON THAT LINK TO SEE A STORY, HAVE YOU? WELL HOW ABOUT SEEING SOME FUCKING POINTLESS ADVERT IN THE MIDDLE OF YOUR SCREEN FOR FIVE MINUTES WITH A TINY X IN THE TOP RIGHT-HAND CORNER WITH A BIT OF TEXT SAYING 'CLICK HERE FOR ARTICLE'? HOW WOULD YOU LIKE THAT? YEAH, YOU LIKE THAT, DON'T

YOU. YOU LIKE THAT. GO ON, TRY AND CLICK THERE. GO ON. SAUSAGE FINGERS. KEEP TRYING. THERE YOU GO. OH, BROKEN LINK. HA! BUT WE'VE MADE A WHOLE FUCKING TEN PENCE OUT OF YOU. FUCK YOU, YOU PIECE OF SHIT! WE WIN! YOU LOSE! YEAH, YOU LOVE IT LIKE THAT. AND YOU'LL BE BACK TOMORROW.

Oh, the article wasn't quite what I'd been hoping for.

Butwhataboutthemen?[47]

January 27, 2011

What about the men, eh? Whataboutthemen? Women are just as bad as men. If not worse. In fact, definitely absolutely worse. Probably. Almost definitely. A woman once looked at me funny and all of that. I think women are horrible, and they give birth to children, and all of those things. (How many words left? OK, pad pad pad...)

Loose Women, they're allowed to sit there and say things about men, which is just as bad as all the misogyny in the entire world; honestly, you have no idea what it's like to be on the receiving end of a sweeping generalisation from

---

[47] This post was loosely based on a Giles Coren article for the Daily Mail on the same day.

Coleen Nolan - you have no idea in the world what it's like. It *hurts*. It hurts like hell. But men are supposed to just sit there and take it, but we're the real victims. We're the real victims because we're on the receiving end of some pretty nasty criticism from women, and that hurts.

I mean, what kind of world is it where you can't just sit around and talk about smashing some woman, and calling her it, and say you're probably going to be hanging out of the back of it? That kind of harmless banter has been going on for years, and there's nothing wrong with it, because it's completely harmless, and if you say it's not sexist then that means it isn't. There's nothing wrong with saying a woman's going to be rubbish at her job just because she's a woman - look it's ironic, because it is, and I've said it is, which means it is. It might not sound ironic but if you look at the wider conversation, you'll see it definitely is, and, well, you probably don't understand because, well, you're probably on the blob or something, no offence love, eh?

Men are the real victims of sexism. I have no actual evidence for this, but it's almost certainly definitely true, because, well, there is no because, but who's going to bung you a few quid for saying that in general it's women who are discriminated against? Come off it! No, contrary to what you may have seen elsewhere, or thought in your own mind, men are the real victims, and you're just going to have to take my word on that. What about the men? We're victims of misandry and hatred every day of the week, but of course you're not allowed to stand up for yourself and say that, because the PC Brigade and mungbeanchewingGuardianistas are going to get all angry and then you're going to have to stand in a corner and wet yourself with fear.

(Nearly done? OK) So, to sum up, men are the real victims, Loose Women exists, and everything is the opposite of what you think. There.

You must never look

January 21, 2011

There's a sobering moment in Werner Herzog's documentary film *Grizzly Man* which is still one of the most haunting things I've seen on film. The director is listening to audio tape of environmentalist Timothy Treadwell and his girlfriend Amie Huguenard being mauled to death by a bear. He is in a room with Treadwell's mother. Visibly shaken by what he has heard, Herzog simply says: "You must never listen to this tape. You must destroy it, and never listen to it."

We can only hope she did what he said. But in less serious matters it's hard to get across a message like that without piquing people's curiosity. How do you say, for example, "Don't look at the comments on anything on the internet ever" without making someone peep through their fingers to see what's so bad? How do you intensify the warning to a seasoned reader of internet stuff, to say "I know it's a cliche to say 'Don't look at the comments on anything on the internet ever' but I really mean it, especially when it's on a Comment is Free article about feminism"?

It's not easy. I tried with my own father when I first showed him a blogpost on his computer.

"What's this bit here?"

"Oh, those are the comments, don't worry about them, don't read them, you know, haha."

And he started reading them, of course. I had to leave the room as I saw the colour draining from his face. Short of pulling the plug out of the computer or frisbeeing his laptop into the back garden, I didn't know what to do. It was like watching someone you love be dragged through a steaming midden by a team of shire horses. It was awful. And this wasn't even one of the bad bloggers - one of those ones (you know the ones) who attracts a team of needle-dicked women-hating scumbag bastards who drool about how female writers "need a good seeing to" and other such delights; this was just an ordinary blogpost.

It's impossible not to look. You can try not to look, but you just end up looking, and giving yourself a sadface. It's the same when people haven't heard of the rum coves I sometimes mention on Twitter - happy-go-lucky Americans, for example, who have lived their lives without ever having to find out about Andy Coulson; or people who are fortunate enough to tweet me with "Who is this Nadine Dorries anyway?"; or, poignantly, those folk who say "Richard Littlejohn, who?"

Oh, the lucky, lucky, jammy bastards. How I wish I didn't know. And I always try to say the same thing to them. I try to be like Herzog in that poignant moment. Don't find out, I tell them. Don't Google them. Don't take a peep around the curtain. Don't look them up and don't read anything about them; and your life will continue as it is now, without a noticeable decline in happiness.

But they do, they always do. And then Pandora's Box is open. Just like your first exposure to the goatse man, you can't undo what's been done. Sure, you can carry on and pretend it never happened, but it happened, you know it happened, and you'll always be left with that mental image burnt onto your mind's eye. I feel so guilty sometimes, about being the first person to pop someone else's Nadine Dorries cherry, or bring them their first ever Littlejohn column. But what can I do? I'm curious too. And it always ends up getting the better of me.

You must never look, I say. But we always do[48].

Samantha Cameron in a bikini[49]

May 30, 2011

I went to the mall. I suppose it's a cliched thing to do on a

---

[48] I don't so much nowadays. It's a much less stressful life. Does that make me a bad person? I don't know.

[49] This post did not contain anything about Samantha Cameron in a bikini. However, there were many pictures of Samantha Cameron in a bikini at around the time I posted it. I therefore reasoned that it would be a good idea to call it that, in order to disappoint my readers with a long-winded and convoluted post, even more than they would already have been disappointed. This kind of thing pleases me.

bank holiday. I don't really know because usually I work on bank holidays - or until now I will have worked on bank holidays, except work is coming to an end - at least, the kind of working that I'm doing now, if you can call it that, and I suppose you can.

(TL:DR. TL:DR. Too Long: Didn't Read. I can feel you stroking your index finger down the mousewheel already, looking at the mountain of text ahead - not that I've written it yet, but I know that I'm going to - and wondering whether you can force yourself to keep going, to trudge through the increasingly stodgy dumpling-like turgidity of prose, without even any demonstrable reward in sight, apart from knowing that you started something and didn't finish it - that you were able to do something and not quit halfway through... for which, many thanks. But TL:DR. TL:DR. Or TB:DR. Too Boring, Didn't Read. Is there some equivalent passive-aggressive gainsaying response? Something like FO:YC? I don't know. That just seems a bit juvenile. And it is a bad thing to be juvenile, apparently, probably especially when it's particularly a temptingly thing to easily do. Telling someone to fuck off is just like putting the letter 'i' in a TO LET sign. It's the obviousness of it that makes it shameful, even if it has an intrinsic humour that taps into a childish part of the brain - it's a toilet! - but still, sometimes the obvious thing to do is the right thing to do. Which is why I did the obvious thing, and went to the mall.)

I read a story today about a rapper I'd never heard of very much, who'd crashed a jetski into a bridge[50]. Which was

---

[50] Sean Kingston.

hilarious and also pitiful at the same time. The idea of someone crashing a jetski into a bridge is funny. Because bridges are quite large things, and they don't tend to trick you by wobbling around very much. There is that element to it: the idea of the silly man crashing into a bridge on a jetski, ploughing straight into it, as if it wasn't there, but discovering that it was, in fact, very much there. But then there's the idea that this is a human being, with a soul and with dreams, just some other person, as real and as bright and as flawed as everyone else, who happens to have driven a jetski into a bridge. I feel sorry for him, although I repeat I hadn't really heard of him very much. I kind of know the name but not a great deal else about him. If you played me something he did, I might have heard it, and I might shrug my shoulders and say "Oh" but that's about it. But that doesn't matter. It's just some man crashing a jetski into a bridge. Like the man who inflated his buttock with a high pressure hose[51]. Funny, but sad really. If he'd blown his head up like a balloon and popped his brains all over the room, I don't think I'd be chuckling as much. But then again, that still is a bit funny, if you're detached enough from that other person, if you can imagine it all like a cartoon, which it isn't. Because he's got a face, and you don't want him to be hurt. Or I don't, anyway, cloyingly sentimental nonsense of a sadsack that I am.

I nearly walked into a concrete staircase when I went to the mall. That's what that last long, miserably rambling

---

[51] This also happened for real. It was a news story from New Zealand that was doing the rounds at the time, due to the buttock hilarity.

paragraph was leading up to. I nearly walked into a concrete staircase, which might have given be a bump to the head, or sent me into the path of a passing car, where I could have been run over and killed. Unlikely, you might say, and you'd be right, but people's buttocks inflate with high pressure hoses. People drive jetskis into bridges. It happens.

And I thought about what people might discover if I had been killed. What would people try and understand about me? What would they look back on and see? Would they look back through notes I'd made in books about being happy, and decide I was happy, and that this was tragic, because I'd seemed happy? Or would they look back through tweets and other things I'd written, and decide I was sad, and that this was tragic, because I'd seemed like I wasn't happy? Or would they look through my internet history and see that I'd spent a lot of the morning looking at 'sexy' photographs by Dave Lee Travis[52] - then what? Would they have thought I admired Dave Lee Travis and his pictures, and found them possibly arousing? "Oh that's sad," people might have said, "But at least he enjoyed those Dave Lee Travis pictures before his accident." And then I suppose they would have said: "I wonder if it's that Dave Lee Travis, you know, the one who got a Gotcha from Noel Edmonds?" And they might have done some searching on Google and discovered that, yes, it was him, after all[53]. "Oh well, at least he saw those nice pictures

---

52 These photographs really do exist. Dave Lee Travis takes slightly erotic photographs as a hobby.

53 Yes, it is that one. Google it if you don't believe me.

before he died." What if that was the last thing going through my head? A picture by Dave Lee Travis[54]. What a thing to be thinking of. But that's how it happens, I suppose. There are no big speeches and sudden exits. One minute it's this, the next it's that.

I suppose the only way you find out any of these things is if you ask. Perhaps that is the sad thing, when someone does drive a jetski into a bridge, or gets blown up like a balloon, or walks into a concrete staircase, or whatever; you don't have the ability to find the answers to the questions. You're always trying to reach out into the void, to think what someone might have been thinking, or feeling; you're always a hundred thousand miles away from knowing what they really do think.

That's why we go to the mall in the first place, to have some kind of certainty in life. Go to the mall. Find something. Find something you might like. You can't have what you do like, not what you really like, so find something you kind of like. I wandered around the shops, and I thought "I kind of like that. I don't mind that. That's nice, but it's too expensive... do I deserve it?" and felt those things that all of us feel, I think, when we do this fruitless kind of comatose hunter-gatherer thing, on a bank holiday, along with everyone else, because it's raining

---

[54] Since writing this blogpost, the news broke that DLT had been a source of inspiration to Aung San Suu Kyi during her exile in Burma. It made me see him in a completely new light. And then I remembered the photos and I carried on very much as before.

and there's nothing else to do. Pick a thing you want. Decide whether you want it or not. Make the decision, have certainty. If you want it, you can have it. If you want to get it, get it. Hand over the money, it's yours. It's for you.

But then, I find it equally dispiriting in those places. I feel so much that it's not for me. This isn't for you. You don't belong here; I don't belong there. All the massive posters in the windows - perfect white teeth, perfect skin, perfect smiles, perfect people. Look at this! Have this! Get this! You deserve this! You're entitled to this! You can have this if you want it! Treat yourself! Spoil yourself! Spend! Enjoy! Be! But then I look more closely at the windows, at the shuffling, awkward, fuzzy figure with baby elephant hair and ill-fitting fat person clothes, and I think: No, this isn't for me. This place is not for me. Where is? I don't know, but not here. And so I leave, quietly, not having bought anything, and that's all right, I tell myself, because I wasn't meant to do that anyway.

TL:DR. That's fine, I don't mind at all. By now you will have given up, having decided you D want to R it because it was TL. You may have even decided to write something in the comments. "What are you doing, writing about this?" you might ask. "I don't think I enjoyed this as much as other things you have written, it's disappointing. It's like you are trying to be difficult and unreadable." But then that's not you talking at all, is it; it's me, telling myself. You could be writing something along the lines of "I haven't read this post but I can't say I agree with it, based on the headline and the first couple of paragraphs, so here's what I think". And you're welcome to that, too, of course. I don't seek out these things. I don't go trawling for controversy. If nothing else, trying to be difficult and unreadable, except with a huge amount of patience and persistence, does delete the obvious path to going trolling around looking for people to annoy, then getting all happy because at least I have attracted someone's attention by being CONTROVERSIAL and CONTRARY and being a real ICONOCLAST so that one day I might be invited onto a television programme to be similarly CONTROVERSIAL and ICONOCLASTIC. At least I haven't done that. And I wouldn't like to do that. And I'm glad I don't. I don't want a billion comments telling me I'm wrong underneath, or a billion and three telling me I'm right. I just write because I write because I write. Sometimes I write for others and sometimes for me; this is very much for me, and I can only apologise for it in advance, if it's not quite what you hoped for, or might have been expecting.

I went to the mall. I came back. I wrote. How am I feeling? Am I unhappy or happy? Am I pleased or dismayed by Dave Lee Travis's pictures, which I have obviously introduced into this to make this whole self-indulgent stain of a blogpost somehow absurd and ridiculous, so I can get in first before you attempt to ridicule it? Ah, I will say, I meant it to be nothing to enjoy all along; I even introduced a minor celebrity's attempts at erotic artworks, as a kind of parallel with my own shambolic amateur-hour efforts at writing something. But you couldn't sell this blogpost for £900 in a lacquer frame, I will tell you that much. You couldn't sell it for anything.

Sometimes, the jetski hits the bridge.

That's it for Enemies of Reason.

Warm Cherryade[55]

I'm a liar

July 27, 2009

"You lie on your blog."

"What?"

"On your blog. I was reading it today and I thought, that's not right at all, he's lying about it."

---

[55] I gave this blog the title Warm Cherryade as I wanted something that conveyed disappointment and a certain kind of banality. I think some of the posts may have conveyed this a little too well. Still, I enjoyed writing the blog, and it sat quite nicely alongside the others, though few people knew that I was writing it, as I put it under my own name. It was quite interesting for a time to see a post that 'Anton' would write getting loads of readers, and one that 'I' was doing attract barely a ripple of interest. I think that's partly because I'd built up quite a loyal and decent readership with Enemies of Reason; and partly because a lot of Warm Cherryade was a load of rubbish.

"Which bit?"

"I can't remember. I just knew that you were lying."

"Oh."

"And all that guff about being a failure, honestly, what's all that? 'Oh I'm a failure, except I want you all to love me and say I'm brilliant, and I can feel like I'm a success on my blog, unlike in real life…'"

"I don't think-"

"…as if you even think that! Arrogant bastard. Sitting there writing stuff to make you sound better than you really are, lying."

"Which bit?"

"What?"

"Which bit was I lying with? Which article was it? Which post? What sentence?"

"I don't remember. I just remember thinking you were lying."

"That's not good enough! You can't just tell me I'm lying, but you can't remember what it was I was lying about, or when you read it, or anything other than I was lying. You can't even tell me what it was I was lying about."

"I don't remember."

"And what did you think of the rest of it, all the other thousands of words that weren't lying?"

"I don't know. I only skim-read it."

"You only skim-read it and all you can say is that you know I was lying, but you can't remember what I was lying about, and you don't remember anything good about anything I wrote – all you can remember is something negative, and that somehow that makes me arrogant and lying because you couldn't be bothered to read the rest of it."

"You're a sad bastard living in your blog world, demanding praise from people who only exist on the internet."

"I don't. I just write things and sometimes people write things back, and sometimes they don't. That's not sad. That's just how it works. I'll put this fucking conversation on here if you want."

"You don't have my permission."

"I don't need your permission, this has already happened. I'm going to write it down and if you disagree with it you can write a comment underneath."

"I don't want to write a fucking comment underneath, I don't want to register on some bloody website just so I can tell you you're lying."

"I'm putting it on the blog anyway."

"You'll just try and make yourself look good, like you'll have the last word."

"I won't."[56]

Cabin Fever

August 9, 2009

I'd never really believed in cabin fever, until now. I suppose you can find it hard to believe in things you haven't experienced. I mean, I'm not worshipping a packet of Ryvita as God or carving pictures of the television set into my arm with a rusty breadknife; none of that's happened yet. Nothing quite so elaborate as that. And besides, it's only been a few days anyway, well OK, a week, since I've been outdoors.

A whole week indoors, ill, with only daytime TV to keep

---

[56] This conversation really did happen, in case you're wondering. I think I come out of this quite badly, but then that was the general idea. The other person involved in the conversation wishes to make it clear that she believes these were not the exact words spoken.

me company. The cat's been no good[57]. Animals are meant to be intelligent, sensitive creatures who can sense when you're ill and come to look after you to make sure you keep them alive. Not mine. She fucked off straight outdoors at the first sniffle, and has only returned for a few bowlfuls of stinky catfood since. Outrageous. But understandable. Who wants to be around a sneezing, wheezing, coughing ball of virus and phlegm? Not any creature with any sense.

Daytime TV though. Christ. I've never seen such evils until now. I swear when I was a kid and you had that magical few days off school to sit around watching TV, there were better things about. Even Afternoon Plus or Judith Chalmers in an orange bikini[58] were better than this. Jeremy Fucking Kyle. I mean, honestly. The man's a menace to humanity. One day, surely, the audience will just tear him limb from limb and feast on his wretched corpse; at least, in my mind, they will. And I hope they broadcast it, as a warning to others not to be weasel-faced

---

[57] Which is putting it mildly. My cat is an evil cow. Well, not cow, cat. But you get the general idea.

[58] Wish You Were Here? Was the title of the programme. This is a nod to Julian Clary in the now-forgotten 90s sitcom Terry and Julian, and specifically the line: "That's nothing, I just saw Judith Chalmers in a tangerine jumpsuit". Hard to enjoy out of context, I grant you, but it still tickles me.

shouty bastards on television. Please? Can we have that?[59]

It hasn't helped, I should add, that the next-door neighbours have been hammering, drilling, sawing and generally making some kind of bloody racket all day, every day, since I've been confined indoors. They've sounded like they've been constructing an Ark; all they've actually ended up with is a wooden fence. Surely an entire week of work should get you something better than that? Was it really worth the effort? All that time, all that possibility, and they've taken down one perfectly good fence and put up another. They should be removed from the earth for having wasted their precious lives. When you're ill you suddenly realise all the things you should be out there and doing, but you can't because you're stuck indoors, and so even seeing someone just sitting around in their garden makes you instantly hate them and want to throw things at them, and shout: "Get out there! Enjoy the world! Do things! Be useful! Use your precious gift of health!" But you don't, you just sit around indoors and feel a bit grumpy.

I mentioned the other day[60] how I felt being ill was a

---

[59] I wouldn't really want to live in a dystopian future in which Jeremy Kyle is murdered live on television. That would be a bad thing. I am exaggerating for comic effect, to be clear. And I want it made clear that Jeremy Kyle is probably a nice person, underneath it all, and does stuff for charity, probably, or something.

[60] warmcherryade.wordpress.com/2009/08/04/sickness-reboot/

chance to take stock, reboot and look at stuff in a slightly different way. While that's still true, now I am just overwhelmed by the desire to get out of the house. I have been sitting in roughly the same place for seven days, looking at the same views, seeing the same things, getting increasingly frustrated that I'm unable to do anything. I'm even starting to miss work, and that's the worst thing of all.

It reminds you just how nice outdoors is.

I gave the spider a lift to work[61]

August 12, 2009

Every day, I give the spider in my wing mirror a lift to work. I don't know what he (or she) does when I'm away, or whether he (or she) even notices that the entire outside world has shifted in the space of an hour or so, but I

---

[61] I can't remember if this blog entry predates me seeing the marvellous Mik Artistik at Glastonbury or not. But if I saw Mik first, then his song 'Sweet Leaf of the North', about a leaf trapped under the windscreen wiper which travels down with him to a gig in London and back again (Sweet Leaf of the North / You go back and forth), definitely inspired me. If you've never heard of Mik Artistik, you must go out and buy an album. Now. Go on. Or just look on YouTube. Then go and buy an album.

suppose it might make a change of scenery, if he (or she) could be bothered to take a look around and see that everything's suddenly altered, and different.

Sometimes I imagine that the spider who lives in the wing mirror of my car might fall asleep before I drive to work, then wakes up when I get home, never actually realising the 86-odd mile round-trip it's been through during the day. Then again, I've seen him (or her) clinging on pretty fiercely and retreating into a safe little nook to avoid being blown away by the air rushing by when I'm on the motorway.

There's something faintly reassuring about seeing its beady little eyes and spindly body sitting there whenever I get back to the car after a day of work. Time for us to go home. Who knows; it might even make me drive more carefully to know I'm carrying a passenger.

You think of these things while you're commuting. It takes away the endless, repetitive tedium[62].

Toast

---

[62] At the time I was driving from Bristol to Swindon every day and back again. Well obviously back again. I began to spend more time on the M4 than is generally considered healthy. If any time on the M4 can be considered healthy. Which it probably can't.

July 15, 2009

Toast has never killed me. I hope it never will. And yet, when I eat a bit of toast, late at night, while I'm on my own, I am struck with an all-pervading fear that I might choke on it and die. What if you choked on it? What if you couldn't call for help? What if you died alone and no-one found you for ages?

Luckily, I have planned to thwart this eventuality. I always chew toast just that little bit more than I really need to, ensuring that it's a minimal choking hazard. I feel secretly proud of myself for being rather cunning.

Also, I've decided that if I started to choke I'd sprint down the stairs and out the front door before attempting to un-choke myself by running backwards into a lamp-post. I reckon I'd have a few seconds, but I could do it.

I hope this kind of fear doesn't become self-fulfilling. I'm sure I read somewhere once that phobic people are more likely to be killed by those things they're phobic about than non-phobic people are likely to be killed by those same things.

Maybe I should just give up toast. That would really make it impossible. Or would it? Someone I went to school with had a premonition he would die in a freak yachting accident when he was 23. He said it'd be easy and he'd just avoid the water until he was 24. But then he was driving down the M3 one day and he saw a ruddy great yacht on the back of a trailer. (He didn't die, but that's not the point).

No, and I can't live my life just worrying about choking to death on toast. It's highly unlikely. Still, if I did, having just written this about it, I would at least have the satisfaction of knowing I had every reason to be fearful just before everything went white and I stopped breathing.

That's a comfort, at least.

Oracle

July 16, 2009

Sad news today: ITV's Teletext is no more[63].

Like most things on British TV, it was invented by the BBC and copied by ITV. Badly. Oracle, as it was then, was always slightly brasher, slightly less stuffy, slightly cheaper-looking than the Beeb's Ceefax. The adverts didn't help, of course, although in later life they provided me with a

---

[63] www.guardian.co.uk/media/2009/jul/16/teletext-to-be-pulled-tv And then, all of a sudden, it was gone. You don't miss what you've got till it's gone, do you? Especially when it comes to text-based infotainment with blocky graphics. You don't miss that till it's gone. And then you don't even feel like you're missing it. But you are. You're missing it. You might not feel like you're missing it, but you're missing it. Admit it, you're missing it. You are, aren't you?

cheap holiday and Peter Kay with a comedy riff[64], so it's not all bad.

The thrill of our first Teletext-enabled TV was quite something. As I recall it, the remote control was the approximate dimensions and weight of a small breeze block, with stiff rubber buttons that attracted all the grease and muck from under your fingernails. A giant red light flashed on the front to tell you that you'd pressed something properly, although if you weren't pointing the remote at exactly the right place, at precisely the perfect angle, and it wasn't too sunny, and there wasn't a shadow over the TV, and the batteries hadn't run out, which they always did, then you could manage to change channels *without ever leaving the comfort of your armchair.*

Not just that, though; the remote opened up this whole secret world of cyan, magenta and green, blocky text that burnt itself onto your retinas if you stared too long at it.

Sometimes they even tried to do pictures, or there were quizzes that you could play along with by pressing the 'reveal' button on your remote control – except it tended to 'reveal' all the answers in one go, so you had to try and look away again quickly if you really wanted to play, or try and answer five questions at once.

Sure, later there was Bamber Bamboozler and the sorcery of 'Fastext', but that was an innovation that kept Teletext clinging on with its fingertips while that new-fangled

---

64 You know, the 'Gorrit, booked it, fucked off' one.

internet started up. There was a time when the ticking over of the page numbers seemed lightning-fast in comparison with early dial-up internet, where you had to remove all images from a page, be around during a time when no-one else was possibly using the worldwide web on the planet and throw a double-six in order to get a single page of text to load. But it didn't last.

Digital TV didn't help. Whereas Teletext's whirring pages stumbling through the numbers 101 to 301 seemed slow, it was positively lightning-fast compared to the can't-be-arsed sloth of digital teletext, which grumbled about doing its chores like a stroppy teenager. Maybe that's what really killed it off. People just can't be bothered to wait for five minutes for the front page to load on Freeview, let alone for a bewildering and unhelpful menu to try and get them around.

Still, it's sad. Those mystical numbers are buried deep into my brain. 101 for Ceefax news, 300 for ITV news. 302 for Ceefax football[65]. 150 for 'Newsflash', which popped up in its own little window on the screen. Russell Grant's Stars. Useless recipes. Pointless quizzes. And now they'll soon all be gone and forgotten, though not quite by me[66].

---

[65] 316-17 for football scores, 324-5 for league tables.

[66] One of my first ever experiences of being published was on Channel 4's Teletext service. There was a section for teenagers which had readers' letters so I wrote in under the pseudonym Elsie Nibbet, who was apparently 108 or

Why you must never give up (aka the pint glass miracle)

August 3, 2009

A cheery story which always reminds me to stay chipper in the face of adversity, illness, disappointment, despair or general malaise. It's set in a horrible nightclub – oh, 'horrible' doesn't really do it justice, but just imagine that every time your shoes pressed down on the tasteless carpet, a bilious ooze of sick and stale beer squirted out[67] – and the date was about 1997. It may even have been 1998, although that's kind of not too important right now.

Anyway, I was at the bar, queueing to get an overpriced pint. Every pint was overpriced. This was London, albeit the grubby suburbs, and this was past 11pm, which mean that if you wanted to carry on drinking, you had to waste money, stand behind a velvet rope for about half an hour in the horizontal rain, and then pay through the nose for whichever pasteurised once-fizzy-now-flat draught lager

---

something. Those were the days. The thrill of being published, the thrill!

[67] I am talking about a horrible place in Harrow, where I was a student for three long and tedious years. I dare say it's still going so I won't name it. But blimey. What a shithole.

they wanted to give you. That was what happened, and that was what you had to put up with. There was no alternative.

I see an eager lad walking through the masses of men – always men in these places, even if women were given free entry it didn't matter… these holes were so dingy that even the most desperate female alcoholics would rather go home and empty a toilet duck than try their luck amidst a lairy crowd of denim-clad nutcases always at the boiling point between guffawing with their mates or shoving a pint glass into someone's eye – and this lad was doing the thing of carrying three pints of Guinness.

I never quite mastered that ability until well into my mid-20s, so it was an impressive sight to see such a young lad doing so well. Or so I thought. Until the foremost glass of the three went tumbling down onto the ground.

His face, I can remember his face. It was a mixture of despair and agony. So close to getting back from the bar! So close to getting back with the precious extortionately expensive booze. But no. Shamefaced, he shuffled off.

I don't know if it was me that saw it first. But someone did. Hands pointed at the magical sight.

The pint glass had fallen onto its base. And stayed there. The liquid had gone flying up into the air, but almost entirely returned back into the glass. In other words, the pint was intact, despite having fallen nearly three feet onto the soggy carpet. No-one had kicked it; no-one had knocked it over. There it sat. I can see it as clear as day right now.

And when this lad saw the miracle, he almost didn't want to pick it up. He wanted to stand there and admire it, as we all did. These were the days before camera phones or most people having digital cameras; there is no recorded evidence except what's in my mind. And to this day I can say, I was there, I saw it. I saw that Pint Glass Miracle.

And that's why you should never give up[68].

Aborted shopping

July 24, 2009

You'll see them all over Ikea, the abandoned yellow bags stuffed with goodies that didn't quite make it to the checkout; in each rough plastic bag there are dreams that didn't come true, stories of anguish and unhappiness and relationships breaking up, and a pitiful world of sadness.

These are the shopping trips that went wrong, or took a

---

[68] In case you're wondering whether this really happened or not, or whether I just made this up as a kind of suburban fable, it really did happen. I saw that pint glass fall and land like that. I saw the miracle. I am here to tell you that this happened. If I achieve nothing else through this publication, it will be to convince you that I have seen a pint glass fall on its base and not topple. My work here is now done, I feel.

turn for the worse. People came in looking for something, and maybe they found it, but it just wasn't to be. They might have had something in mind to buy – they went as far as to take items off shelves and prepare for purchase – but no, it didn't quite happen.

It's particularly in Ikea, I think, that you'll see these forlorn little yellow lumps of regret dotted around the store. More than in other shops, although if you've worked in retail you'll know that objects find their way around the aisles and go walkies every now and then; you'll have seen abandoned baskets of groceries just sitting there, begging to be taken home.

But what is it about the Swedish furniture behemoth[69] that makes it especially prone to aborted shopping trips? I believe I have an insight into this phenomenon, having slouched through my local outlet this morning. Like others, I had every intention of getting something. Like others, I wanted to go through with it. But then, something happened; something changed, and I just couldn't bring myself to finish what I'd started.

There's something about going there in the first place that fills you with dread and revulsion. Maybe it's the memories of long-buried spousal arguments over bed linen or storage jars, the scars making themselves known as your eyes scan the dismal concrete car park for signs of

---

[69] I say 'behemoth' but originally I'd put 'monolith'. I prefer 'behemoth' to be honest with you, which is why I've changed it here.

humanity, and find none. Maybe it's the dreary inevitability of the whole thing, as if there's nothing you can do except go through with the meandering shambles of brightly-coloured plastic and shiny metal with their jolly faux-Swedish names, thinking that you're saving yourself a million pounds' worth of time and wages whereas in reality you're just creaking around a clanging, gloomy, rain-lashed warehouse with just-too-bright spotlamps, with the torrential cloudburst battering the tinny roof and creating a hubbub of grumpiness.

Whatever it is, you just can't be in there and be cheerful. No-one comes out of there beaming with delight. It's just a case of having got through an ordeal, like stumbling down the steps of an aircraft after experiencing heavy turbulence mid-flight, or walking out of A&E with a friend or loved one. It's a sense of shared terror gradually dissipating; a sense that what went horrifically wrong might just be all right again, one day. People look around, and blink at the sunlight, and say to themselves, *well, I have lived, and I have been through this, so things cannot get any worse.*

Once you're in there, you just want to get in and out as soon as possible. But it's not always as simple as that. You'll be stuck behind ditherers weaving across the aisles with their trollies full of nothing; you'll be bashed and bruised by impatient growling couples trying to patch up their floundering relationships with a bit of redecoration; you'll be thwarted by the confusingly bleak layout of the place, which makes you feel like you have entered somewhere which is endless, which will swallow you whole, and which will never let you out.

Maybe it's the length of the queues at the tills that make people decide to abandon their shopping and get the hell out of there. That's one explanation, but I don't think it's entirely that. Because today, this very morning, laden with goodies in my bright plastic yellow bag, I was confronted with the shortest Ikea queues I'd ever seen. Literally one or two people. I could have paid for it all if I'd wanted it, and it wouldn't have meant shuffling in line behind a dozen or so fellow sufferers.

No, it wasn't the queue. So what was it? I think it was just a suspicion of angst creeping around my brain, clutching at my face. It was a sense of "What am I doing here, buying this rather ordinary-looking blanket for £29? Is that what blankets really cost? Is that really good value or am I just getting something because I'm here, because to not get something would feel like I'd wasted my time going out of my way to be here?" or something very much like it.

When you do abort shopping, there's something quite naughty about it. You know it's wrong, but something of the excitement of bunking off school or taking a day off work to go to Alton Towers starts bubbling up inside your chest. Why not just leave the bag there, and get the hell out, and leave? Why not do it? Why not run out into the fresh air, and leave, without having paid any money at all? Go on!

And so you do. You find somewhere quiet to leave the bag, and you place it gently down on the ground, and you start walking to the exit. Every step makes you feel even better about your decision, and all the money you've saved.

It's almost like un-shopping. And it feels pretty good.

Farewell Prozac[70]

Some things you just can't fix

October 29, 2009

It's good to be able to fix things. Good, but you can't

---

[70] As you may have guessed, I wanted to choose a different name for the blog, to call it 'Goodbye Prozac' or something, but I couldn't find the right title that hadn't already been taken with a Blogger blog. So Farewell it was. As it turns out, of course, it wasn't farewell at all, but I wasn't to know that. I wrote these posts at a time when I had decided to try and come off antidepressants; I was also undergoing psychotherapy – I say 'undergoing' there as if it's an ordeal or something, but then that's the word my brain selected, so that's the one I'll stick with, I think. So I was in a place where I was constantly reflecting on things and trying to analyse what was going on, always talking about my feelings; and I felt that writing a blog might be some kind of help to expiate some of the things I was thinking and feeling as well. So that was that. Since I'd written about depression on Enemies of Reason, it seemed natural to carry it on as 'Anton Vowl' – but these posts would be so different it made sense to put them all somewhere else, and that's what I did.

always. In those moments of severe depression, and feeling low, it's easy to think that everything boils down to you being unable to fix things, and that you are powerless to change anything for the better. Powerful enough to make all the mistakes you made, of course, but powerless to decide everything else that might happen.

That's not the truth, though it's a convincing and convenient narrative when you can't understand why you're feeling so low. So much easier to blame it simultaneously on yourself and the world: I've made everything wrong; and everything is stacked up against me, and I can't do anything about it. The worst of all possible everything[71]. But that's not how it is.

There are the minor things that go wrong - the annoyances, the irritations, the tiny mistakes, and they can add up of course. And then there are the things where your fate rests in someone else's hands - the job you didn't get, the promotion you missed out on, the people who don't really want to be your friends, the others who treat you unfairly, or unfavourably, and get away with it, and

---

71 Sentences like this read a bit clunkily when you see them on the page, but I rather like it that way. With Farewell Prozac the idea of the blog was that I'd just write each post in one go, rather than thinking about it over any kind of time period; I'd get an idea in my head as to what I'd write about, then when I was ready, off I'd go, without stopping, until it felt like I'd written all I'd wanted to write. This was a liberating way of writing, much less studied than some of the media analysis stuff at Enemies of Reason, and something I really enjoyed doing.

there's nothing you can do.

And of course there are, too, the things you remember, the things you couldn't fix, the things you couldn't do anything about, but which are ruined, and wrong, and which make you feel completely powerless and totally alone. An ambulance. A hospital corridor. The smell of the disinfectant. The whirr of the morphine[72]. A face you recognise, but don't recognise, because it's so different, and because it will never be the same. A particular morning, cloudy, overcast. The clothes you were wearing. A phone call. You can't change these things. You can only experience them, and they will hurt you, and that will never change, and it's going to keep coming from now until forever.

A lot of my depression came, and still comes from time to time in those moments where it feels awful for a few seconds, where the heart sinks and the stomach kicks you, where you get transplanted to another time and another place, and you're on the wrong end of the telescope[73], and

---

[72] As I later wrote about in the post 'Making peace with places', this refers to the death of my mother, from cancer, in 2000.

[73] I know this is a bit of a cliché, but it feels so true that I think it's beyond a cliché and is actually the right thing to say. There's a bit in A La Recherche... where Proust's character talks about the death of his beloved grandmother, the sense of suddenly being alone, suddenly realising that you live and die alone, and that's what I was trying to get at. There are moments when you do feel incredibly small, and incredibly

the world is unimaginably huge and bleak, from the frustration of not being able to change things.

But. And there is a but, before you think I'm dwelling in unhappiness. There are other things to remember too. That you were strong. That you managed to cope, despite everything, and that it made you bigger, and better. And that even the thing that hurt you the most, the one thing you wish you could change if you could change anything - that one defeat you can't ever forget about - didn't beat you. It didn't see you off. It tried. But you could take it on, and you won.

A few weeks on, things are still going okay for me. I thought I couldn't do it, and I didn't know if I could, but I could, and I am. And there have been times - many times - when I thought it might just be easier to forget about all this, and to carry on with the medication, and see how it went, and that wouldn't be so bad. And it wouldn't have been, and it's not necessarily the wrong thing to do, but I didn't do that; I've kept going, kept trying.

And things go wrong. A mistake here, a problem there, a failure or two. Things that don't go my way, and I have to try and look at them and think: I've seen off worse. And I have. Do I need medication? Not now. There was a time when I think I did, and I probably did, but not now. You don't need to be fixed, because some things don't fix, and some things can't be fixed. Sometimes you just have to be as fixed as you can be, not perfect, not undamaged, but

---

alone, and the death of someone you love is one of those times.

still all right.

I'm still strong.

A little cry

September 24, 2009

It's probably a scenario that goes on more often than you might think. Given that it's entirely a private affair, we don't know the extent of it, but I'm sure it's happening right now somewhere, and no-one else knows about it.

Sometimes we all get a bit teary. I'm less prone to this than I think I should be, really, but then there's no way of knowing how often people do get that way. All I have to go by is the people I know, but then I know how much I hide from them, so it's not very easy to judge.

But, every now and then, it happens. I don't know if it is anything to do with the coming off antidepressants making me a bit more sensitive, or whether I've just had a bad week anyway - which happens - or it might be the fact I was back in my home town at the weekend, which brings a few unwelcome feelings and memories pouring back into my mind[74]; but whatever it was, I suddenly felt a little

---

[74] I have written about this a lot, returning home and being confronted with a lot of uncomfortable feelings. I think

bit weary yesterday afternoon, and felt the need to be on my own for a bit.

The toilet cubicle at work - there's something so banal and frustrating about the location that it probably makes it easier for you to be in touch with those childish emotions that make you cry: the frustration, the despair, the foot-stamping it's-not-fairness that you tried to abandon when you were about four years old but has still lingered around ever since, no matter how much you've grown up in other ways.

There, behind the tasteful formica walls, you can blub away as much as you might like, with the flush as an emergency sound to mask the involuntary heaving of your chest, should someone else go into the room. A private little space that's meant for catharsis, albeit in a more fundamental sense than just releasing some salt tears, but it'll do. No-one can see you, and you can just relax into it for a few minutes, and dry it all away.

And then you emerge from it all, back into the world of work, the same indistinct rattle of keyboards and hum of computers; the same trilling of phones and murmur of conversations. And you look around and you realise that you've managed to conceal it from everyone, again; you've managed not to show them you're weak - you've managed to keep that mask on for a little bit longer.

Next time, you might not be so lucky, and someone might

---

nowadays I've managed to reconcile a lot of this, and I feel a lot happier being back.

catch you with a tear in your eye while you're on the stairs or something. There's always that danger. But at least, for now, you can be perfectly alone in it, isolated away from all those human beings around you, without needing to explain anything. And that's quite a comfort, in a way, not having to expose that vulnerable side to anyone other than the people you really want it to. Whether we like it or not, it's easy to be marked down as that crazy person, that overemotional person, that mad person. Better to hide it all away, and keep it from them. Then they'll think better of you.

And so, I did. And that was that. And today, I don't feel so teary - just a bit sad that I do get that way sometimes. But I do.

No need to panic. No need to worry that it's something going wrong. It's not something going wrong; it's something necessary. But still, above all, something secret. A little cry. Forget it and get on with your day. Be strong, even though you're not[75].

---

75 There was a recurring theme through these posts of the idea of 'strength' or being 'strong'. I don't really know whether that was the right thing to be thinking about, at the time, but it was the place that my mind went to when writing the Farewell Prozac posts. I was trying to think of myself as a 'strong' person if I could carry on and give up antidepressants, while I would be a 'weak' person if I finally crumbled and failed. That was the idea, anyway, though I don't think it ended up that way at all: I think it's stronger to realise when you are helpless. You're strong when you realise

My last cigarette[76]

September 29, 2009

Last weekend, on Saturday morning, without fanfare or drama, I swallowed what will hopefully be my last ever antidepressant tablet with a mouthful of orange squash, looked out of the kitchen window and then got on with my day. It was an entirely unremarkable act which means nothing unless I find that I'm able to cope without it ever happening again, which is what I hope.

I'm aware, of course, that addiction to something as pervasive as nicotine is an entirely different pair of trousers to the kind of discontinuation syndrome associated with SSRI antidepressants. But I wonder if there might be some way of drawing parallels between the two. Having what might turn out to be my last antidepressant reminded me of the day I had my last cigarette, and how that marked a similar change in my life between everything that was before and everything that was after. Sometimes these things happen, and they do mark a change - not the towering epiphany of predictable fiction, but an event that really does mark a difference

---

you're not strong. You're weak when you think you're strong, when you're not. If that makes sense.

[76] I smoked Marlboro Lights for about 10 years, and loved it very much, apart from the coughing and knowledge of self-killing.

between one time and another.

It was January, and if I remember correctly I think that there were still Christmas decorations in the windows - I'm pretty sure there were. I'd been suffering with a virus, which was gradually getting worse and worse, although I'm not really the sort - or should that be, I wasn't really the sort - to make a fuss about my health, and I just tried the age-old masculine way of dealing with feeling weak and vulnerable: to plough on through it, to imagine it isn't there, to look strong when you feel weak, just to make sure that you don't attract a stray piece of pity on the breeze.

It was pretty cold outside, and I was walking back from the bus stop, having seen off a friend who lived on the other side of London and who needed to get home. I felt like a cigarette, even though I'd been coughing a bit, and sparked it up. It was almost impossible to inhale. I just remember the smoke lingering around in my mouth like dirty brown waste, curling about my mouth and nose as I struggled to force my breath out around it. There was no way I could even smoke. There was just cough after cough after cough. I had to stop and sit down for a moment, by the side of the road, because I was a bit dizzy. You know, nothing serious, but just felt like a little rest. And I managed to get home, boiling hot and cold sweat at the same time, all the time the breath struggling to puff out between the lips.

Cough after cough. What was going wrong? I remembered an age-old asthma diagnosis which I'd completely ignored a few years before; that was a long time, and a lot of cigarettes, ago, and nothing that bad had really happened to me. Cough after cough. Breath becoming shorter. Maybe I should lie down? That's what it felt like. Just lie down and you'll feel a bit better. Sleep for a bit, you're tired. Then it will all be OK. Breath getting shorter. Coughing. Short breaths. Heart thumping, jumping, jittery. Sweat. Dizziness. With every short breath it all got worse, with every time the lungs struggled to force the air out and in, it kept feeling worse, the slight pain in the chest, the tightness, the coughing, the puffing, the dancing lights.

Something was wrong. Sometimes you just get the idea: this is wrong. This is too wrong not to do anything about it. So I called an ambulance, which arrived a couple of minutes later, and then I was on it, sitting or lying (I can't remember which) with a mask over my face. Then there was a cold bit of air between the ambulance and the hospital, and I was in a wheelchair or on a trolley or something, and there were people looking at me, and I was a little more awake. Someone took blood out of a vein, and an artery, which made me feel queasy as I looked at it stickily jetting out; then there was quietness, just the hiss of the mask, the faint cool wisps of smoke around the face, and the breathing became longer, and then I returned to life, not that I'd ever gone, and maybe I'd never really been in danger, although I always do wonder what might have happened if I had decided to go to sleep, and I never really know.

Then there were hours spent quietly in the hospital, behind a curtain, listening to snatches of other people's conversations, seeing the odd bloodied face or body getting wheeled past. Did I want to call anyone? Did I want to let anyone know I was here? No. No, I didn't. I wanted to just be alone, so no-one knew what had happened; I wanted to be perfectly isolated, to be away from it all. And the doctor said, you really shouldn't smoke any more if you don't want this to happen again.

And so I didn't. I chucked the cigarettes in the bin on my way out to the taxi, which drove me home in near silence. The sky was lighting up with a greeny grey dawn, and one or two Christmas lights still flashed and buzzed on the sleeping houses. That was it. That was as close as I'd ever been to death, and it made me feel appallingly alone. It made me realise: it's the only thing you ever really do on your own. When it happens, as it might, you might realise what's going on, or you might not, or you might think everything's going to be OK, and it won't be, and then there will just be shining corridors, and hushed voices, and that will be that, and the curtains will be drawn shut around you.

There was no such defining moment to tell me that I had reached the point where it might make more sense to stop taking antidepressants. There was no sudden realisation, no epiphany of the kind that don't happen in real people's lives[77], no drama, nothing like that. Just a desire. Just a feeling that it might be the right time, and that I might be ready, and that I might just have sorted enough shit out to be able to cope with this.

I don't know if it'll be the last. It'll certainly be less dramatic than my last cigarette. But that's no bad thing. Instead of being forced into making the decision by being

---

[77] I'm constantly trying to write about the idea that there aren't such things as epiphanies, but this event would appear to be one. Even though it is, it isn't; it's just something that marked a turning point. It wasn't a sudden realisation or a lightbulb going on or anything. Perhaps it was just the time for these things to happen, I don't know.

scared, I made it on my own, in a positive way. It won't be as significant a moment as quitting smoking, probably not, but it might be more worthwhile in the end.

The void

October 1, 2009

I don't know if stopping these prescription drugs will leave me with a void where they used to be, or whether everything else will just fill the space that was left behind. It's hard to find hard and fast rules, because everyone's experience is so different. In the end you end up coming to the conclusion that you can't really come to a conclusion, because you're not the same as these other people, your experience isn't quite the same, that so many other factors are different in your life, and a million other reasons why everything is still unknown.

But if there is to be a void, it won't be the only one that I have. You come to terms with the absence of things, the absence of people, and although other things come along, and other people come along, there is still a void, a void of emotional expectation if nothing else, a jigsaw piece that other piece will fit - a shape that reminds you where something, or someone, used to be[78].

---

[78] Again, as I'm writing this I suppose I am thinking about Perec – the void in the missing vowel (or Vowl), and the jigsaw puzzle piece theme from Life: A User's Manual.

We all have these voids - the schoolfriend who moved house, and whom you never saw again; the friends you meant to keep in touch with, but you didn't; the exes you said you'd still be friends with, but aren't; the people you miss, because they aren't around any more. They all create voids, and you realise the voids are there when you think of their faces - the way they spoke, or their handwriting, or something as simple as how they looked when they were angry, or upset, or cheerful, or their face was contorted with laughter and the tears ran down their cheeks, and the tears ran down your cheeks too.

It's not so hard when you know that person is out there, somewhere, living their life blissfully unaware that you remember them, or maybe even aware, but as unable to contact you as you are to contact them; and sometimes it's better that way, because some people belong in a certain place, in a certain time, with a version of you that was maybe younger, or more naive, or less easily tired, or whatever. Maybe we keep an idealised imago of the people we lose touch with, and that suits us, because it means we don't have to see them again, and recall their bad habits, or faults and failings, or the things that frustrate us about them. Sometimes, though not all the time, it's better to remember those people who exist only as voids as the parts of them we liked the best. Sometimes you lose touch for a reason, and when you go back, you remember why, and it's disappointing.

But of course there are other reasons why there are voids. Sometimes you don't choose for people not to be in your life, but they go anyway, and there's nothing you can do about it. Most of us, as we get older, carry around the voids of others who have left us because they died. I know I do - so many more than I would like to have.

Grief itself is something that can lead to depression, I think, or a welling-up of feelings that can tip you into that way of being. A sense of hopelessness arrives, which overwhelms all those frustrated feelings of wondering why, of trying to work out how, of trying to understand those things that can't be understood - what it is that takes the wise and leaves me behind, someone so much less wise, someone so much less good. It's not just coping with the void itself, but knowing that the void will always be there; that you will always have to live as someone who has had someone precious, only to see them die suddenly - or, perhaps worse, wither away in a long drawn-out battle with an illness they couldn't ever hope to win, but tried anyway.

You begin to look at yourself and question yourself - you can feel guilty or responsible, though those feelings tend to fade away as you accept there were some things you could never change; but they're replaced by feelings of uselessness, when you realise that of course someone else's death wasn't your fault, because nothing very much is your fault, because you don't have the power to control other people's lives, and they will suffer and be hurt and die and there's nothing you can do about it. That can lead to depression too. When the one thing you want, more than anything ever, is for the person you love to stay alive, and you can't do anything about it except hope, and that hoping isn't good enough, and you're not good enough, and you don't get what you want, because this isn't about you and what you want, or what anyone wants: this is just about what happens, and you're just a spectator among many millions of spectators, not the protagonist in some grand narrative.

And then you have to come to terms with the fact that

your heart will always be broken. That you will always have to associate a person you loved with feelings of grief as well as everything else you remember; that their void won't be the optimistic, rosy one you choose for those people who drifted out of your life, but one which is, no matter how full of cheerful and happy memories otherwise, always tinged by the fact you know how their story ended, and you know that it's ended for good.

Then there are voids that come with grief in other ways. It's realising that a person you relied on for love - unconditional love, in the case of a parent - and support, and everything that comes with that, won't be there for you. It's a selfish feeling that comes after all those that reach out to the person who has gone: it's where you realise that they can't be there for you again, despite all that they've taught you, despite all that they did for you; that they won't be there, and can't be there, to share anything else with you in the rest of your life. You can look up to the clouds and imagine they're looking down on you if you like, but you know they aren't, not really.

But if you can live with that - and I have for a while now - then you can get stronger because of it. If you can keep going, even when there is no-one to support you and no-one to help you, at least not the person you always went to for support and help, then you realise that you're stronger than you thought. If you can live with that, no matter how much it hurts and no matter how much you wish every day that things had been different and people who are gone were still around - if you can keep going despite all that, then leaving a void of medication starts to look like a much easier prospect, almost trivial in comparison, although it isn't. Just as when someone you love dies, you find love and support from other people, even though it's not the same, but you accept that it never will be; then when the support of medication is gone, you can look for that support from elsewhere, and probably get it too, if you feel ready to. And I do.

We all live with voids. My life is not especially tragic or sad, just as tragic or sad as yours is, or anyone's is. It just so happened I lost a few people a little earlier than I should have done, or hoped to do, and I always wish they could come back, but they won't. Maybe that is what made me strong, not what made me weak. Maybe that's what gave me the kind of strength to finally be at the point where I can feel like I'm going to beat depression; not what caused it in the first place. It's hard to get to a place where you can get to think like that. So hard. But maybe I'm there now. Maybe the voids don't hurt. Maybe they give you strength.

I finished the Farewell Prozac blog, thinking that the work was done and that I'd finished, but it didn't quite work out that way, as the next post describes.

These are some Enemies of Reason pieces dealing with depression which I've hived off from the main section – it just seems to make more sense to have them here. I'm sorry if it seems I'm rabbiting on about depression all the time, but there it is; these are the pieces I keep coming back to, and which seem to have had – judging by the reaction of readers – the greatest impact.

Besides, depression is a thing that exists in you, whether you like it or not. It's not just a question of feeling a bit fed up or being unhappy with the way things are – although they can be around as well – it's something beyond and below all of that. It lurks around. It runs through you like the colour in marble. It's just in you, and it's hard to get it out. I have tried self-help books, and therapy, and antidepressants, and self-medication, and pretty much everything I could have thought of to make me feel less depressed; but none of it has 'cured' me and I think nowadays that it's just there forever, and I can only hope to take the edge off its unpleasantness as best I can, and keep riding the rollercoaster. And I'm fine with that. Well not 'fine', but you know.

FAIL[79]

April 1, 2010

I had to try. I had to see if I could. But sadly, I couldn't. Things didn't quite work out.

I think if there's one word that sums up how we view things nowadays, it's FAIL. You don't quite get what you want and it's FAIL. You don't achieve what you set out to, you FAIL.

Someone else doesn't understand what you're saying: FAIL. Fail, fail, fail. Sometimes it feels like we are trapped

---

[79] This was an Enemies of Reason blogpost but it makes more sense to put it here, given that it's relating to all of the Farewell Prozac stuff.

in a binary world between WIN=1 and FAIL=0. Sometimes, it's not quite that simple, I think, though it certainly feels like a FAIL for now.

Regular readers, bless you, might have guessed what it's a fail about. The rest of you might just have to bear with me while we plough through all this messy personal stuff; if you're not interested, then I really don't mind, by the way - we'll pull our ripcords and float down to Littlejohn-joke Island[80] sometime tomorrow morning, I imagine.

I know some people think you shouldn't write about personal stuff, or that by writing about it publicly you somehow make it worse; but I don't really listen to that at all, and I don't think it's right, either, for what it's worth. This is, I think, what blogging is about - putting yourself into the story, or into what you write, rather than seeing yourself as a camera taking stills of the world. (I see as I write this that yet another "Is blogging journalism?" debate is being kicked around on Twitter at the moment, which I'll happily not be touching with the smellier end of

---

[80] I use this phrase quite often and you may well recognise it as a nod to Bill Hicks and him telling his audience that they'll all pull their ripcords and float down to Dick Joke Island, when he was introducing them to material they may not have been expecting. I get a sense of that with the blog sometimes, that sometimes I'm not writing about stuff that my 'readers' will be interested in; but then, on the other hand, a blog is like that: sometimes it's not going to be stuff that you agree with, or stuff that you're going to necessarily expect. That's something about blogging I really enjoy; you can feel as free as you like to confound expectations as much as possible.

a shitty stick.) One of the things I like about blogging is that it's the expression of yourself in relation to the things you see, and hear, and feel, rather than a simple snapshot of the world, imagining that you're capable of detaching yourself from it. Then it's important to say who you are, and how you feel, from time to time, or as often as you like, I think.

So, to the failure. Well, it's like this. Turns out it wasn't quite goodbye, or farewell, after all, I'm afraid: because this morning, after a lot of thinking, I gave up giving up. I started taking Prozac, or fluoexetine, or whatever you like to call it, again[81].

FAIL.

I don't really know what made me start again. It's a combination of things rather than one specific event. But generally it was this: everything just started to fall apart, a bit. Unfortunately, but there you are. Everything had seemed to be in place - as in place as it was ever probably going to be, I think - but I couldn't quite string it all together. Or perhaps I just should face up to the fact that

---

[81] I'd had a particularly bad birthday and, just as when I wrote about the incident of giving up cigarettes, I don't want to think of re-starting antidepressants as an epiphany, but yes, it does mark a turning point. It does mark the point where one thing ended and another began. Maybe it's only writing about these things that makes them epiphanies, but I still refuse to believe in them, or people's own narrative arcs, or fate or destiny, or anything like that.

having to take medication is something that I'm going to have to do, just like I take it for other things in my life, and that this is no different, and all the counselling or therapy or whatever else you might try in the meantime isn't going to change all of that. Is it time to face up to that, now? I suppose so. But I would never have known if I hadn't tried. You've got to try, otherwise you'll never know, and you have to know, so you have to try.

I feel disappointed, but not crushed. A little bit hurt, but not beaten. Low, but I've been lower. This isn't as bad as it could be. As I always say, it's only through learning where you're vulnerable that you learn where you're strong. I remember reading once that they knew where to reinforce planes that came back from the Battle of Britain because those were the bits where there weren't any bulletholes. It's only through getting hit, and surviving, you know how strong you really are. It's only through trying, and failing, you know where you succeed, and how you can do better.

It's how you deal with it that counts. I'm not weak.

The rather odd thing is that yesterday I got some good news, the best news I've had in ages. Someone actually paid me for something I wrote - the cheque arrived, and no, I wasn't dreaming, it had actually happened. In a strange kind of way, perhaps that makes you look at things differently, when you hit your goals, even in a small way, on a small scale, in a way that matters not very much to anyone else at all, but means the whole world to you. WIN, you might say. The day didn't end up feeling full of WIN, but it doesn't always matter how things end up; what matters more, perhaps, is what happens next.

So what does happen next? I just carry on. A lot of things seem to have fallen apart and taken a knock - another thing that's gone wrong, to add to the list of things that have gone wrong? No, not really. Just a little fail. You don't need the capital letters. A little fail and a little win, within 24 hours of each other. Perhaps that's it. Perhaps if you can belittle the triumph, as much as you can the catastrophe, into as small a thing as you can make it, that makes everything small stuff, manageable, something you can deal with. A little fail, a little win. A little of each every day, it needn't add up to anything sinister, or problematic.

And knowing that you might not be strong enough to cope on your own? That's not a fail. That's strength over time - the strength to realise when you can't cope, and admit you're vulnerable, and need help; better that than blundering blindly along determined and stubborn, and ending up getting really hurt, or ruining things for those you love most.

Don't worry, jokes tomorrow. For now, a pause. It doesn't feel as bad as I thought it would do. It feels OK. Relief, if anything. And now, with help, and the love of those around me, to get the rest of it sorted out. And I will.

Farewell Prozac, one year on[82]

September 20, 2010

As you might know, about a year ago I started writing another blog called 'Farewell Prozac', describing my attempt to try and get myself off antidepressant drugs. So I thought I might write another post now, with a bit of hindsight, to look back on how it all went and how things have progressed since then. This is one of those blog posts that you might find either entirely pointless or quite enlightening, but I make no apology for it being either, or neither, or nothing at all.

Looking back, it was an optimistic time and things appeared to be going well. I remember the feeling of being able to adjust to life without drugs, and then all the problems that came - but there was a long period of feeling fog-bound and disoriented, as if I didn't really know what was going on, where I began and where the drugs ended. Eventually though, that was it, and I felt that things were going well enough that I stopped the blog, as it seemed there wasn't anything left to say.

Later, I eventually realised that I wasn't coping well enough without antidepressant drugs, and so I started

---

[82] Again, this is an Enemies of Reason post but it belongs in this section. I thought it was important to look back on the whole thing with the benefit of hindsight, which we bloggers perhaps don't always do.

taking them again. As I said at the time, it was and wasn't a tremendous fail; I felt like a failure, because I realised that I couldn't cope without drugs; and I felt like I wasn't a failure, because at least I'd realised, rather than carrying on without it all and thinking I was going to be all right, even when things were going wrong.

Re-reading the Farewell Prozac blog, I rather like a lot of the writing, and I find it a lot more enjoyable than, say, some of the old blog posts on here, because there's still something that I can connect with, something personal and human, something quite emotional and quite raw. I like all of that, even if I don't like remembering all the reasons why things went wrong in the first place and why they kept going wrong, and how I couldn't quite succeed in the little task I had set for myself that I felt would make me able to deal with life more easily.

How do I feel now? I don't feel better, not completely, and I am kind of resigned to the idea that I might have to continue taking antidepressant drugs for some time to come yet, maybe for all of the future - but it's not so much resignation, perhaps, as just feeling like that's the right thing to do. Perhaps by attaching a status of negativity to being 'on medication' that we put pressure on ourselves to come off it at some stage in the future, in a way that we wouldn't with medication to help with things other than mental health problems. Maybe it's only by dealing with that that you can find some kind of tranquillity about the whole thing, some kind of peace with yourself and your situation.

The place where I am now is a much better place, I think, and maybe that's just the reason why I don't feel under pressure to make any changes. Things are going well. I have found things to occupy my brain and stop the restlessness that caused such anxiety in the past; I have my writing to entertain me, and occasionally others, as well; and I have support from a lot of people who mean a great deal to me. Nothing is perfect, of course, and there are so many things I would change, but then so many things I wouldn't change, either. I am getting to a place where it all seems all right, after all.

I suppose the thing I have learned from all this is that you might not be able to achieve the things you set out to do - like giving up antidepressants, for example - but you might be able to achieve something of value through doing it. I still quite like reading that blog, after all. I mean, there are loads of things wrong with it, and loads of things that make me wince to read, but I don't really mind at all - I did it, and I finished it, and that's that. And when you look at things with a bit of hindsight, as I am, a year on from starting that blog, you can notice that sometimes the trajectory is upwards, and sometimes things do improve, and sometimes you do feel like you're making progress, and you feel like you might just have a chance to end up somewhere good. And a chance is all I need, because I am going to take it.

It gets better[83]

December 20, 2010

Things get easier. It gets better.

I'm not trying to patronise you or tell you something you don't already know. I don't think I'm better than you, because I'm not. I know you might not want any advice, or help, or anything. I know you might feel that there isn't anyone out there, anyone who can help; that things have gone beyond the point of being helped; that things have gone wrong too often, too deeply, and that it can't ever be brought back. I don't know you, and I don't know your situation. I don't know how you arrived here or what brought you to this point. And I am not an expert, and I don't know what to say, but all I do know is that you're here now, and I hope you might continue reading. Please just give me a moment.

---

[83] This post was written after I wrote about having discovered that many people had landed on the blog while searching for 'painless suicide methods' thanks to an old post I'd written about an entirely unrelated subject; the post was entitled 'Suicide is painless' which is what had brought so many people to the blog. So I wanted to write something for anyone who did land on the blog because of those search terms, because every time I thought about what it must have taken for them to do that web search, it made me feel awful about the consequences of using a throwaway line as a blog title; I wanted to try and do something positive about it. And so here it is.

It gets better. It does. It can, and it will. It might not get better today, or tomorrow. But it will. It can, and it will.

Yes, it might be that it gets worse again, I won't lie. The 'getting better' bit doesn't end up soaring into the sunset, leaving every problem and trouble behind. Things don't magically disappear, never to return. Things keep coming back. Sometimes, the same mistakes keep happening. But there is time - time for things to improve, time for you to accept the things that hurt so much, time for things to change, or not seem so bad as they do right now.

I know this because I've been where you are. I've been there. I have felt something like what you feel. Not the same as you, not in the same circumstances, with the same problems, or the same worries, or the same background as you, because I would never presume to think anything like that. All I know is that I've been there, at that place in their minds that people go to when they feel like they can't carry on. I have been there, and I have felt that all was lost, that nothing would ever improve, that nothing would ever get better.

I don't know what it was that helped me to fight off those feelings. I am not a strong person. I am a weak person, a failure in so many ways, a loser, a nothing, a nobody. I'm nothing good to anyone, and I have made a million mistakes. But if I can say I managed to do anything, it would be to have fought off those times in my life when I felt that things had gone too wrong, and that I was overwhelmed by the desire to sleep, and never wake. I am not strong, but I fought.

You might feel like you can't tell anybody what you feel,

that you might be judged, that you might be thought of badly. That's understandable. But once that first word leaves your lips, or you manage to write down what you feel, and tell it to someone else, you will feel relief. You may want to speak to someone you trust, or someone who doesn't know you at all. There are all kinds of places where you can go, and you don't have to confront anyone, or be judged by anyone, or be thought of differently by anyone. There are people who love you, who care about you, whose lives are changed, and improved, and made better, by the fact that you're around; and there will be many more in the future.

You're not alone. This isn't how things will always be. It might feel like that way now, but this is not forever. This is only now. It might feel that you are living in the eternal present, without being able to see the future, trapped watching the mistakes and humiliations and pain of the past repeat itself in front of your eyes in your mind. But this is not forever. This is not how things will always be. You are not doomed to live in this moment forever. There will be another hour, another day, another week. Maybe take it an hour at a time. A minute at a time. Let time pass. It goes so slowly when you want it to pass, but it passes. All things pass.

I have been there, and felt those things. I have felt like it wasn't worth continuing. I have felt it would be better if I weren't around, that the world would be a better place, that I would be better off dead; I've felt like it would be the right thing to do to just end all the pain and the misery by ending my life.

It doesn't change overnight. There are small changes at first. Take baby steps. One thing at a time. And things might go wrong, or feel desperately bad, again. This is just the first moment towards recovering from how you feel now. But it gets better. It does get better, I promise, it gets better, there is so much more. Remember laughing till you cried. Remember feeling warm, and secure, and loved. Remember the things you've done that made others feel happy, that you did just because you wanted to. Remember the good things you've done. That isn't too far away. That hasn't gone forever. The bad memories are more seductive, more inviting; it's easy to cling to them and think that is all life has been, and all it will be, but that isn't the whole picture. It gets better. It can, and it will.

I can't tell you that your life will change, or that you will change, or anything like that. All I do know is that there was a time, not so long ago, when I felt that there was no escape, no option, nothing to do but end everything. I felt that there was no alternative. I felt there was nothing else that could be done. And that was that, and I wanted it all to stop.

I didn't stop. I kept going. It's got better. It's got easier. Not easy, because it isn't easy. For some of us, life is more difficult. For some of us, everything is more difficult. That might be your situation, or it might just be what you're going through now that makes you feel the way you do. But no matter how much it hurts, the hurt lessens. It doesn't fly away, never to return, but it begins to hurt less. Every second, every minute that takes you further away from this moment is something to treasure, and enjoy. Every second and every minute you fight this feeling is a victory, a little victory, but a victory. Take it a minute at a time, then there will be one day at a time. Then there will be a month, another month, a season, a year. Things will change.

I can't offer any magic or any solution. I can't offer you anything to hold on to other than hope. There is always hope. When hope seems like it's all gone, it still remains. It never leaves, and will never leave you. Hope will never leave you. There is a glowing ember, a fire in your blood, the oxygen that burns, the fire of life. Keep it burning.

I am, and I'm not[84]

January 19, 2011

"Hello, notice of possible redundancy," I said, the brown envelope sitting softly in my sweaty hands. "We meet again, after all these years." And there it was.

Someone once described it to me as like walking through a cornfield and having a pool table land on your head, and I suppose it did feel a little that way; except my pool table has been hovering for a while - when you see so many others in the same industry, and others, going through the same thing, it's not a terrible shock - but it winds you, all the same.

---

84 At the time of writing, I'm still redundant. Well, still imminently redundant. Perhaps things have changed since then. Perhaps I have a new and fantastic job. We'll have to wait and see. Hope it's chips, it's chips... wait, that's something else, isn't it.

Last time, I avoided the redundancy, but ended up a gloomy, self-absorbed opaque puddle of sadsackery and introspection - wondering why I was going to end up on the scrapheap in my 30s; why I'd chosen to funnel myself into a moribund career choice when the signs were obvious that the comet was going to hit; why things had all gone so wrong so quickly. I kept the job, but I didn't really keep my composure. In a funny way, this time around offers an opportunity, of sorts - to be able to deal with it better, and more maturely; probably, what I'd like is to get a small payout (it'll only keep me in pies and gravy for a month or two) and not to be so stressed out by it all.

You get a sense of time, sometimes, when things are ending. I recall a moment of clarity I experienced while having a Little Chef Olympic breakfast at motorway services while on the way to the last ever football match I covered for a newspaper I used to work for; there was a palpable sense that one thing was finishing, and another was beginning. Now, today, I get the same feeling, looking around the drab, charmless office where I work - a sense that I won't be here much longer, probably - and, perhaps, that something else might be starting.

People start to look at you a bit differently. Like you're a half-blind old sheepdog panting away in a vet's waiting room, waiting for the needle, or something. They don't want to make eye contact; suddenly they don't need to know you so much, or maybe they're embarrassed and feel a bit sorry for you - in fact, it's probably the latter. The same sense of awkwardness, just about something else.

Something ending, and something beginning. Last night I went for a walk, and the stars seemed very bright, and full of hope. There are better things coming, I thought to myself. Better times ahead.

In the meantime: gissa job.

Making peace with places

February 5, 2011

Sooner or later, when you come stumbling through your 20s if you're lucky, or your 30s or later if you're unlucky, or just not quite able enough to have got to grips with these things earlier, you have to make peace. Make peace with people, and situations, and feelings that you have; and, as I've found out this week, with places, too.

I've always had the feeling, when coming back to my home town, of a weight pressing down on me, of things having been left unfinished somehow, unsatisfactory, of there being things that needed to be tidied away. I didn't know why that was, and I'd largely tried to forget about it. I moved away when I was about 26, which was a pretty good age to do it - move away, get away, leave everything behind. For those of you who stayed around, you probably did all the dealing with things earlier, I think; moving away gives you breathing space, a chance to forget, a chance not to be reminded maybe, but everything still is there, waiting for you, whenever you return. And sometimes you don't have to return physically; sometimes you're just transported back, through memories, or dreams, to that place where you grew up, where you used to live, to that place where there are ghosts.

I only ever go back home to see my dwindling family or my friends, the people I went to school and work with, and I don't hang around for long. A pint at Christmas; the chance for someone I vaguely remember from school to insult me and try to start a fight with me for no plausible reason; the chance to dwell over all of those missed opportunities, could'vebeens and neverweres. But this week, there was the chance to make peace with one particular place, a place which has (or possibly had) a kind of gravitational pull on all the other places nearby, over all of my home town and all the people there.

It's a hospital. We all have places that have horrible things associated with them, and I'd never been back, not since... well, not since then, a particular day a few years, many years ago. I hadn't been back and I hadn't wanted to be back. But by a strange coincidence, I ended up going back. Not for me, but for someone else. And so, there I was, driving to the same hospital, seeing the same ghosts. Faces in corridors. The shining floors and clanging open spaces. The whiteness. The emptiness. And one room, one room in particular[85].

Of course I'd said it wouldn't bother me at all[86]. That's

---

[85] The writing here reminds me of Independence Day by Richard Ford, where Frank Bascombe / the narrator keeps telling readers that there will be a hospital, a corridor, and that only bad things will happen – one of the most powerful pieces of writing I've ever read, and which clearly I had in mind when I was writing this post.

[86] I didn't actually go into the hospital, just dropped my girlfriend off outside as she had a job interview. It was just

just what you say when you do these things because that's how you're meant to feel, but I didn't know what I'd feel. I just hoped it wouldn't bother me. And there it was, and I was looking at it, this building, which had held such awful memories, where things had happened, where people - someone - had gone but never left... well they had left, after all. And what did I feel? Nothing. I didn't feel anything. It was just a building where I was driving someone to a job interview. It was just a big building.

But until I'd gone there, until I'd been back, I hadn't known. That place still had some kind of wariness within me, it still held a memory of grief, and pain, and everything that goes along with it. Until I'd gone back, and then I realised that those things don't always linger; the building is just a building, it's just a place, a place where these things happen, a place where people go, a place I'd now made peace with, somehow, because all the feelings I'd had there weren't attached to it any more.

Once that had happened, everywhere around it began to look different, as well. I walked around the shopping centre in my home town, the awful, drab, identikit shopping centre in my home town, looking at the faces of the people walking past, and they seemed ordinary, normal, devoid of anything that could upset me. I walked around past the empty shops and the sad faces. This was no more the place that could get to me in that way, where

---

the going back at all that brought everything back. I didn't want to say that anything would affect me, because I didn't know whether it would or not.

I used to be, a place from my past that still made me feel difficult, or awkward, or unhappy; this was just another place, a place where I was, a place I was walking around. This was just the same place, slightly different, where the people were older, and I was no-one. I didn't see anyone I knew; I didn't see anything unusual. This was just nowhere, anywhere, somewhere. "Nothing, like something, happens anywhere."[87] That's how I felt. This was anywhere.

And I drove around to the house where I used to live, and that felt like nowhere, as well. It felt like no-one's house. It felt like it wasn't somewhere that belonged to me, where I should even be. And that was that. I was sitting in the car, with the rain falling, the windscreen wipers squeaking across the glass, the engine running, the radio on, and there was just an absence of what there had been. There was an absence of some kind of hostility that I still felt, some kind of resentment, some kind of anger. It had gone.

---

[87] This is a nod to the Philip Larkin poem I Remember, I Remember – which involves him passing through Coventry on a train and recalling his rather unhappy and unepiphanous childhood. I love Larkin and, as with Richard Ford, I love the idea of a writer who hates epiphanies. Banality and bathos is where it's at.

Killing Anton

Well, not 'killing' Anton, as such. But then again, just as I go to delete those words, I think to myself: *maybe that's not such a bad way of putting it, after all.* Because Anton did really exist, I suppose, in some way or other; he existed as my literary persona, as the person I chose to be when I was writing things for the internet and the blog; it's just that it wasn't my name, is all. And he and I were very much the same person. I am not Anton, and he is not me; but we are pretty much exactly the same.

So why does it matter? Well, you have to accept a certain amount of criticism when you choose to have a pseudonym, or an allonym, in my case; you have to realise that people are going to say that you're just hiding behind a silly name, and that you're not really being a real person, and are just allowed to get away with all sorts of naughtiness and nonsense because you are, to all intents and purposes, just a cipher, just a blank vessel, chucking your words out into the ether from the safety of your bunker; you aren't putting your self, or your reputation, or your personality, behind them.

And there's some validity in that, of course, although I think it's one of those increasingly clichéd things for the mainstream media to snipe at anonymous internet folk as if they're all some giant hotpot of hatred, all the same kind of vicious coves who end up littering online newspaper comments. I don't think that's fair at all. Nonetheless, there is a point to it, namely: are you hiding? And if you are, why?

Well, I think I was hiding, and I reckon I can pretty much just come out and admit that. I was hiding, for so many reasons. I didn't want people that I knew to read the stuff I wrote and think of me as some kind of stupid ranting foam-flecked shouty wanker on the internet, as I felt it might make them think the less of me in real life. I know it's a fairly weak argument, but it's an argument that seemed to sway me at the time. What would friends and family make of me if I spoke out so loudly under my real name, rather than an assumed one? Would they just think of me as some kind of idiotic showoff? Would they think less of me? It was a bit of a worry.

But it wasn't just that. I was hiding because of the way I see myself, most of the time, the way I think I really am – this study in mediocrity, this symphony of wasted talent, this collection of random thoughts drawn together to make an unsatisfying whole, trapped in a dull, soft, flabby body, beneath a face that can't look you in the eye. That's what it was really about, I suppose. That's why I liked being someone who was aggressive, in-your-face, argumentative, irascible, all those things I chose not to be in real life, all those things I wasn't quite brave enough to be, and all those things I probably still am not brave enough to be.

It was an interesting double life. I could batter away at my crumb-coated keyboard at work, under the humming striplights, listening to the whirr of the fans in the computers and the occasional ringing telephone. No-one knew what I was up to or what I was thinking. No-one knew that I was secretly writing and broadcasting out to the wider world, sending my thoughts out in the middle of nowhere, into the ether of the blogosphere, or whatever you want to call it. I suppose I was just communicating, or trying to communicate. Meanwhile, I kept myself closed off to those around me, for fear they might spot something about me that would lead them to realise that I was Anton, and Anton was me. That was the uncomfortable part.

There's another part of it, too, that brings all these elements together. Because of the mediocrity of my career, the lameness of what I had achieved in my professional life, I felt like such a fraud judging all these other journalists on what they were writing and what they were doing. How could I, a failure of a sub-editor parked on a grubby desk in the middle of the provinces, dare to bring any kind of judgement on those who had achieved so much more than me? Wouldn't it just be seen as sour grapes from me, taking potshots at those who had managed to secure more of a foothold in the national press than me? I feared it probably would, and quite possibly with good reason. What a fraud I felt. There I was blethering on about media ethics and getting things right, while subbing crappy 6cm nibs about car fucking boot sales. Jesus, what a fraud. What a loser. I could imagine the hot face of shame when I was discovered, and when I was outed. What would people think of me? How dare I pass judgement on others, when my own career had been so poor and so unrewarding! That fear made me want to hide even more.

And one other thing held me back: the talking about depression. I could do so really honestly when I was behind another name. To talk about mental health under your own name, admitting your own shortcomings, or failings, or deep depression and so on, is quite a thing, and something that even now feels hard to do. It was easy to open up about depression and so on when I was being Anton, but it's a sight harder when I'm being me. But I am me, and there it is: I am a person who's got all these various and many problems. I can't hide from that any more, either. I have to try and admit it, and admit that it's me, and that's who I am.

It was strange for me, being two people at the same time, or rather having two personalities. One was the obvious, ordinary, 'real' me, the person who is painfully shy, awkward and difficult to get along with; the other is the 'fake' me, the persona I wanted to be, my Second Life avatar if you like: here was someone who was everything I was not. Here was someone who was confident, assertive, aggressive, and would say exactly what he wanted. There was the freedom, and there was so much pleasure in that duality, for the time that it lasted. But I knew that it couldn't go on forever; there was something corrosive about it as well as something liberating. I wanted to just be me, regardless of whether it would open me up to ridicule or not, and I wanted to stop 'playing a part' by writing under another name, whether they were my words or Anton's words or just my word's under Anton's name, or whatever. I had had enough.

It's strange, really, to think it's a big deal, or was ever a big deal. You might be reading this and wondering why on earth it meant anything to me, or why I might ever have been concerned by it, and I can completely understand that. It seems so insignificant, so unimportant; but then, when I was there, in the midst of it, it seemed so very important. It was all about my identity, and whether I could be brave enough – if brave is not too hyperbolic a way of describing a simple act of being myself rather than writing under a silly assumed name; and I rather fear it is an exaggeration, but there it is, I've written that word, and, as a blogger, I am loath to delete it – to just write anything under the name Steven Baxter. My real name. I wanted it to happen, but I wondered about whether everything would fall apart, my stupidly constructed, oh so vain house of cards, if it did.

If it did happen, I thought to myself, I wanted it to be at a time of my choosing. That time finally came. I was getting fed up with being two people, or trying to juggle two similar but slightly different personalities; why not just be one, and stick with it, and see where it goes? So that's what I did. There was a blogging conference in Bristol, I was asked to attend as it was just up the road from me, I did, and I came as Steve, rather than as Anton Vowl. And there, that was that, it was all over, and all done. I followed it up with an article on the Guardian's Comment is Free site about why I'd decided to do what I'd done, and then everyone slowly began to find out.

My worst fears weren't realised, of course. Everyone was so kind and supportive. I remember that feeling most of all, and the feeling of being accepted. That made me quite amazed. I suppose you think up all these worst-case scenarios and you end up expecting the worst to happen, even though it's not really likely to happen. People were kind, too, about the depression thing, and I felt like I wasn't being judged too badly, or badly at all, come to think of it. People are, on the whole, a lot kinder and a lot less vicious than I fear they are. But as I've said in relation to the way the tabloids stoke up and prey on fear, it's such a powerful feeling: when it's there, it's hard to shake, and your perception of fear seems all to real, so much more real than what's actually there.

There were so many reasons why I couldn't just be Anton any more. I felt like it wasn't being completely honest. I wanted to be honest in all the things I would write about, whether they were uncomfortable personal things or not;

and to do that, I needed to be honest about who I was, and where I was coming from. I needed to be honest about where I was coming from with media criticism and media blogging as well, to tell anyone reading that I had a vague idea of what journalism is and was, whether or not my own adventures in my chosen career had been successful or not; but that I was also approaching the idea of media criticism from the point of view of a punter rather than a professional.

And I wanted to be honest to my friends and my family, to all those who deserved honesty, to everyone who I felt I was kind of letting down by staying hidden. I had told a few people of course what I was up to, but it felt a little odd not to be able to tell everyone. Not that I wanted to go up to people in the street and say "IT'S ME, I'M A BLOGGER!" but that it just made more sense to be able to include it in Steven Baxter's life, rather than a life belonging to a name of someone who didn't even exist.

So Anton had to die. And I had to kill him. It wasn't his fault, and he served me well. But my name is my name, and it makes me who I am. It's my family name, and the name my parents gave me, and it's a good enough name for those who love me, so it should be good enough for me to have for the words that I write. Words that I wouldn't be writing if it weren't for their love and support, in so many ways.

So that's why. I had to kill Anton, as it wasn't fair on me, and it wasn't fair on other people either. I know not everyone agreed with the decision, but there it is. I felt it had to be done, and since it has been done, things have got better. I have felt more confident about my writing – more self-conscious, definitely, but more confident. No, this is me. This is me writing this, in my own voice, using my own words, saying what I want to say, not what some exaggerated blogging caricature wants to say in my place. That makes it easier to write, not less easy, I've discovered. You can just let the words flow, and if they succeed or fail, they are yours, and you have made them. That's a pressure, but it's also a relief. A relief.

Prolls

I wrote a few posts about prolls and prolling at Enemies of Reason but none of them really satisfies me enough to put it here in its entirety. But it's something I've encountered again and again, an interesting phenomenon – certainly not a new one – that keeps popping up time after time in the effluent of mainstream media which I dive head-first into, without a snorkel, from time to time, or which gets thrown over me when I least expect it.

I use the word proll, a hideous neoportmanteauism (do you see what I did there? Oh, you did) combining pro and troll, which I think I may have made up (though someone will doubtless slap me across the knuckles with a boingy plastic ruler and tell me that they thought of it back in 1973, or something) to describe the kind of columnist who doesn't really think anything and just tries to stir things up to get a bit of attention. They're just being a troll, but they are also the original poster; it subverts the logic of trolling, that process of stirring up trouble on internet comments in which the troll says something offensive/provocative/annoying just to grab attention and irritate others, by being proactive rather than reactive.

It's true that what offends is also what amuses. I don't mind that. I don't mind people occasionally or even regularly stepping over the boundaries of what is and isn't acceptable in order to make a joke, even if it's a cheap shot. That's fine by me and I don't mind it at all. I'm not sitting on some ivory commode passing judgement on the rest of the world, condemning everything that isn't terribly clever as being unworthy; that's not me at all. In fact I like a cheap laugh as much as the next person – probably more so. I once spent an entire afternoon practically weeing myself with laughter over some pictures of vegetables with childish words next to them (e.g. BUHTATURZ[88]).

It's not the offensiveness that I mind; it's just that I think it's offensiveness for no purpose other than to be controversial in itself. It's not holding a controversial opinion for reasons of integrity, or genuine conviction; it's being controversial to be controversial, to be talked about, to be 'that controversial person'. It is to be contrarian not because one has thought of all the evidence and arrived at a contrarian position, having gone through the counterintuitive route, but to be contrarian and stab a fork in the eyes of received wisdom (or, more frequently and irritatingly "What some people (usually on The Left) are saying") just because. Just because you can.

"Whatever X says," this attitude holds, "I will say the opposite, I will think the opposite. Whatever Y does, I will say that's wrong and the truth is the opposite. Not because I think so. Not because I care. Just because I want to be challenging; just because I want to be seen to be contrary and adversarial."

I understand why it's done, don't get me wrong. I know it's done to flog a few papers and to create a hubbub; it's done to create a stir and to get people talking; it's done to 'fly a kite' and see who thinks it looks pretty (or ugly, it

---

88 Here it is: www.urlesque.com/2010/09/10/foods-misspelled-names/ - BOK BINS. Genius.

doesn't matter). In the online world, it's done to attract a mass of clicks to your website, even if those hits come from people who hate every single word you're saying – it doesn't matter! You're not going to tell your advertisers that you're getting huge traffic from angry liberals annoyed by your terribly provocative and spiky anti-liberal columnists; you're just going to show them the numbers.

It's just that I find it vacuous, especially when it's done without any style, or with little entertainment value. To be provocative is often a good thing. To be offensive can have a purpose. To be challenging, or contrary to orthodox thinking, or heretical, or counterintuitive, or whatever you want to call it, is very often a good thing. But I don't think the vast majority of the stuff that gets churned out every week, all these uber-spiky opinions dumped on readers like itching powder down your pants, is anything other than wasteful dreck designed to shout and holler and demand attention.

It's what blogs are so often accused of doing, of course, and I'd be insane to think that I've never stooped that low myself. I'm pretty sure that there have been times when I've written stuff that looks pretty like prolling. I hope I haven't been that cynical, that I haven't committed such a professional foul, but doubtless there have been times when I have, and I'm ashamed of it. Because it is beneath all of us to debate in these ways, to think that we can get the most attention by shouting the loudest; we shouldn't think that it's those who get the most attention who are the ones most deserving of praise.

To write provocatively and well, and to write about things you really believe – there's something that few of us can achieve. But it's worth striving for, I think. What it means is that sometimes you're not going to be able to take up the uber-controversial position on a subject, and what you end up writing might seem a little stodgy in comparison to the fireworks and vim of the prolls. But I think that might not be such a bad thing. They might get all the attention, but a huge amount of it is negative, and they're not held in any great regard. If bloggers can get something right – and I actually think this is something that blogging can do very well, and often does better than the mainstream – it's in being thorough about arguments without necessarily running on for 18 pages; to be prickly when needed, but only when needed, to be intuitive as well as counterintuitive, and to actually go along with the status quo, if that's what you really think, and what you really believe.

Because if you end up throwing a lot of rage just to get someone to look at you, you're not a million times better off than a poo-chucking monkey in a zoo, I think. And there I go, ruining everything I've just done with a silly comparison. COLUMNISTS ARE JUST POO-CHUCKING MONKEYS, SAYS BAXTER, WHILE THROWING POO, THE DISGUSTING HYPOCRITE, WHO IS NO BETTER THAN THOSE WHOM HE SEEKS TO BELITTLE AND DEMEAN WITH HIS SO-CALLED WORDS. But I mean it. And if writing, political writing, blogging and columnising is going to mean anything – if it is to have any integrity for readers, I think – it has to be more than "Here's this week's terribly uproarious and nasty thing that will get under the skin of those horrible lefties/righties!" or whatever.

Some people say "I must be doing something right to get so many people angry." Well, not always. Sometimes it just means you're getting it wrong, very wrong. And worse than getting people angry is disappointing them – people who might otherwise agree with you, but find that they wince when they look at your words, because of the thunderingly callous way in which you've put your case.

What I'm trying to say is: just shouting doesn't do any good. You have to mean what you say, and say what you mean, and get it across. Sometimes you need to give people a good shoeing because they deserve it; sometimes people deserve compassion, even if you suspect they're knaves, because that's what makes you better than them.

(Is that controversial enough? I hope so. I mean, I can go back and call everyone a worse name, if it makes it better. Hmm, maybe I should. Maybe that won't make me this week's Twitter hate figure for the Left and therefore won't get me a billion hits to my column, thereby validating what I've written. OK, let me try a bit harder. Er, everything I said, but worse, yadda yadda yadda, Twitter is evil, everyone on the Left is an idiot, political correctness has gone mad, something about disabled people, something about women, whichever is the opposite of what people are expecting to read, regardless of what I actually fucking think because I don't actually think anything for myself, there. That should do. Now, just sit back and watch everyone give me all that attention. Me. Me. Me. Because it's all about me.)

I think the thing is that pro-trolls, or prolls, or whatever try to be surprising and iconoclastic and controversial, but end up being predictable, dull and completely expected; there's only so many times you can deliberately fail to see the point of something in order to throw things at the same old targets before it begins to pall. It starts off being edgy, but ends up being pipe-and-slippers. But somewhere in between money changes hands in order for the 'controversial' pretence to remain.

Life after newspapers[89]

When Fleet Street Calls

When I was about 17 years old, I found this in a dusty old bookshop. It's a funny, battered old thing, but there was something about it that appealed to me. It's called *When Fleet Street Calls*, it's from 1932, and it's by an author called JC Cannell who was a journalist for the *Daily Sketch* newspaper. I used to love writing as a teenager, as I still do now, and the idea of reading about a proper old school Fleet Street writer, with a little press ticket in the brim of their hat, seemed wonderful.

It's a lovely old book of memoirs by a journalist writing in the heyday of newspapers, the 1920s. JC Cannell had a pretty interesting career – he saw the aftermath of the R101 airship crash over France, he was in Dusseldorf to report on the vampire serial killer there, he travelled by air at a time when it was beyond the dreams of most people, and he had a pretty varied career at home too.

---

[89] This is a slightly amended version of a talk I gave to Bristol Skeptics In The Pub on February 24, 2011.

JC Cannell was also a magician – he's best known for writing the definitive contemporaneous book about Harry Houdini. And he used that knowledge in his journalism assignments. He should be something of a hero for sceptics as he helped to obtain the first ever recorded confession by a medium, admitting they were a charlatan and a fraud, and he wrote a lot of articles about ghost stories, mediums and hoaxes, from a magician's point of view, i.e. a rather sceptical one.

One of the reasons why a lot of mediums were believed at the time seems quite charming to a modern reader. Mediums were often elderly ladies, deliberately sweet in nature, who during contact with the spirit world, would spout forth the most disgusting language possible. JC Cannell recalls:

> *A "spirit", using the medium's vocal organs, let forth a torrent of the most obscene language which Mr Ayling had ever heard, although his experience of Army life, I understand, was extensive.*
>
> *"Who was using this vile language?" Keith Ayling asked me. "I do not think it possible that the angel-faced, white-haired medium could have known all those words. Do you think so?"*
>
> *I shrugged my shoulders and said I could not answer for the vocabularies of white-haired ladies.*

It seems amazing now to think that people would be convinced, on the strength of an old granny swearing, that they must be in touch with spirits, but there it is. But you can see in Cannell's reaction some kind of skeptical reaction, the shrug of the shoulders, the looking beyond the obvious and trying to work out what's really going on. To me, I think that's what journalism is, or should be.

The book had quite a big influence on me, and I think it was a large part of the reason why I decided I wanted to become a journalist. It seemed like an exciting life, going to the scene of events, reporting back to your readers, challenging the official version of events, digging for facts, showing no fear, writing on the hoof, being part of something credible.

Of course when I finally became a journalist, many years later, it was somewhat different from the 1930s world I'd read about in When Fleet Street Calls. There wasn't the same excitement. There wasn't the same passion. And there wasn't the same scepticism or credibility.

Looking back, when I first became a journalist, after a year in college and three years at university, it was a disappointment in all kinds of ways. No-one ever seemed to leave the office; reporters and sub-editors alike were chained to their desks, chuntering away on telephones, never really making contact with real people. Was this what working at a newspaper was really like? Apparently, it was. But I did love the job when I started: I loved the way you could use language in headlines and captions to try and play around with the reader's expectations, and I loved the freedom to express myself whenever I got the chance to write something. I learned a bit of discipline and a bit of craft. But I also learned that working for a newspaper – at least the kind of newspaper where I ended up working – was not the glamorous life of the *Daily*

Sketch writer.

JC Cannell existed in a world in which journalists were largely respected and trusted. Newspapers were a lot of people's only news source, and they worked hard to ensure they got things right, even the popular papers. They often broke the news to commuters and readers at home, rather than any other medium. People might not have believed everything they read, but they didn't always have the means to check that what you were saying was the truth, or anywhere near the truth, or not. I suppose that brought about a kind of responsibility on the part of the reporter and the publisher alike.

You tell someone you're a journalist nowadays and they instantly mistrust you, and I wonder what's changed from then to now. Maybe it's always been this way; the phrase 'tomorrow's fish and chip paper' has been around for a long time, and still exists, even though fish and chips aren't sold in newspaper, and even though most of us don't buy a newspaper. But it implies a certain kind of cynicism towards what's on the inky page. But beyond that, I think our view of journalists and their credibility is something to do with scepticism, or the lack of it. For example, while JC Cannell wrote a series of articles debunking mystics and mediums, nowadays journalists are happy to use them when required:

> *(Daily Star front page from January 7, 2011: I KNOW WHO KILLED JO YEATES)*

There's a psychic's word used as if it's genuinely new evidence, not just someone making it up. And this kind of thing is happening more and more – with missing people like Madeleine McCann, or Shannon Matthews, these people are interviewed and treated as if they might have some insight. Because that makes a story, whether it's complete garbage, and insulting and distressing to the relatives, or not. (In the case of Shannon Matthews the psychic actually turned out to be right. Stopped clocks and all that).

Here's a murder, the most serious crime you can get, and it's being treated like a circus show, because here's a psychic, someone who claims to have special powers, who is taken at their word because it creates a story: it is what is known as 'a good tale'. Why spoil a good tale by pointing out that these supposed powers haven't been rigorously tested? Why spoil a good tale by explaining that there's no evidence that this person's opinion is any better than any random guess from someone off the street? No, don't spoil a good tale: just let it flow, and reap the benefits from the readers you might attract with it. Is it about whether it's right or not? It doesn't matter. If that means using a psychic as a trusted source, then so be it.

It's not just psychics who get an easy ride. Most newspapers employ someone to make stuff up every day, in the horoscopes section. Some of these people are among the most highly-paid journalists in the country, if you can call them journalists. And I know it's easy to dismiss horoscopes as a bit of a laugh, as a bit of fun that appears on the puzzles page or next to Fred Bassett and the cartoons or whatever; and I can see that point of view – but it still seems to me something fundamentally dishonest that's going on. The point isn't that readers are being hoodwinked, because they're not, and I'm sure that the vast majority of readers regard horoscopes as being nothing other than mindless entertainment; but when it spills over into news coverage, then it becomes a problem, I think. I KNOW WHO KILLED JO YEATES… Because I saw it in my mind. And these claims treated as credible.

Journalism has a credibility problem, which is another reason why newspapers are struggling and people are seeking out other sources of information. You could say journalists get a bit of a bad press. Of course it doesn't help that some parts of newspapers don't reflect the truth at all. And some parts are just plugging outright rubbish.

But this is all part of the credibility gap. Readers are sophisticated animals of course and know the difference between a horoscope and an editorial on the next page telling them who to vote for, or a report of a murder trial. But I think it's symptomatic of how newspapers have changed since JC Cannell's time, from breaking the news to telling readers what they want to hear. Most of us get our news from elsewhere nowadays, so newspapers have had to change. That isn't working, and sales are still declining, possibly because of the way in which newspapers have changed. It's possible that in the next 50 years there may be no newspapers at all in the UK.

Whether we like it or not, newspapers are dying out and becoming less popular. I want to look at why that is, and what we're going to miss when they're gone. I wanted to try and understand why we fell out of love with newspapers and why people don't trust you when you tell them you're a journalist.

The ghost train

While broadsheet newspapers broadly attempt to tell you what's going on, tabloid newspapers are often like stepping on a ghost train. Fear is the key, but it's a temporary kind of fear. You can read your paper - hoodies are going to kill you, drugs are going to kill you, cancer is going to kill you, immigrants are going to take your job, and kill you - and then put it down, and the real world doesn't seem so scary in comparison. It's a bit of a thrill ride. And people subject themselves to this, quite willingly. People like to scare themselves. They like to read about what's going to kill them this week. They might not necessarily believe everything they read in these scare stories, but they seek them out all the same.

Perhaps it's got something to do with the readership. A lot of newspaper readers are older people, who perhaps are quite scared of immigration, of hoodies, of young people, of technology, of all of that; perhaps the newspapers are just writing for this kind of reader, rather than attempting to present an approximation of what's really going on. Which I suppose is understandable from a business point of view, when you're trying to cling on to declining readers and trying to motivate them to buy your product – perhaps fear is a good way of getting them to pay 40p or whatever for your newspaper. And the biggest fear of all, of course, is death. Which is why there are so many stories about worst-case scenarios, multiple deaths, and deaths from diseases, death that is coming to get you, whether you like it or not.

What's the king of the scare stories? The cancer scare story.

List of things that give you cancer[90]

This is a classic newspaper story. They are the gatekeepers of information; they tell you what a survey or a study or a report says; you must sit there and read it - and be scared. As a reader, you're a passive participant in this, waiting to be scared, waiting to go around the ghost train. Something in a story somewhere says that some cells on a slide might be slightly affected in some way, in one test. Therefore: TOMATO SAUCE GIVES YOU CANCER. Or whatever it is that week. Maybe it's KETCHUP PREVENTS CANCER. It changes from time to time.

Here's a good example. Here are two headlines about the same scientific study.

> *Headline 1: NO PROOF OF MOBILE CANCER RISK, MAJOR STUDY CONCLUDES*

> *Headline 2: LONG CONVERSATIONS ON MOBILE PHONES CAN INCREASE RISK OF CANCER, SUGGESTS 10-YEAR STUDY*

I would ask you to guess which headline comes from the BBC report and which from the Daily Mail, but you're there already. But why did this happen? Well, for one thing this was journalism by press release. We don't know

---

90 You can find these at kill-or-cure.heroku.com, the Facebook group 'The Daily Mail list of things that give you cancer' and the Facebook group 'The Second List of Daily Mail things that give you cancer.'

how the journalists went about compiling their stories or how they arrived at such different conclusions about the content, but in a way, both approaches are wrong. Because no-one writing about the paper had any way of knowing whether the press release accurately reflected it or not – it hadn't been released yet.

I think it's telling, though, that, as ever, the Mail ignores the part of the press release that says there's no proof of a cancer risk, and goes straight for the crumb that says there might be a suggestion that there is. Because it's a better story. Even if it's not accurate, it's a better story. So that's the one that gets told. It's a better story because it's a scarier story: it's the one about death, it's the angle that says *this might kill you* rather than *this might not kill you*.

Another kind of scare is about immigration – it's another fear, another scary thing to be frightened of when you're riding in the ghost train. One thing I've looked at a lot at my blog is immigration stories and the mythology that develops around immigration. Migrants eat swans, for example. This story started happening around the accession of the former A8 European countries to the EU, when Polish and other Eastern European immigrants were allowed to work in the UK without the same restrictions applying as did before. Fear about immigrants isn't necessarily a racist or xenophobic story type in itself; for our island nation it goes alongside other fear stories about invasion or contamination from overseas, for example:

> *VILE-SMELLING FOREIGN LADYBIRDS TO INVADE HOMES THIS WINTER (Daily Mail, November 1, 2009)*

THE PACK OF MUTANT BLACK SQUIRRELS THAT ARE GIVING BRITAIN'S GREY POPULATION A TASTE OF THEIR OWN MEDICINE (Daily Mail, April 26, 2008)

GIANT SEA SLUGS THAT SQUIRT TOXIC INK INVADE BRITAIN (Daily Mail, October 26, 2007)

INVASION OF THE PAINTED LADIES: A BILLION ARE SET TO SWAMP US, AND 10 MILLION LADYBIRDS ARE ALREADY HERE (Daily Mail, July 26, 2009)

PLAGUE OF HAIRY CATERPILLARS WHICH CAUSE RASHES, HEADACHES AND BREATHING PROBLEMS INVADES BRITAIN (Daily Mail, May 30, 2009)

INVADING OUR COASTLINES, PLAGUES OF JELLYFISH WHICH CAN PARALYSE SWIMMERS (Daily Mail, June 15, 2010)

PARALYSED BY THE VOLCANO (Daily Mail, April 16, 2010)

VILECANO (Mirror, April 17, 2010)

There was a similar panic last spring when the volcanic ash cloud from Iceland was demonised and even anthropomorphised into a scary person invading us from the abroad[91]. But you can see how it's all one kind of story – these things are alien and foreign, they are invading, they are taking over, there's nothing we can do about it. Just as flying saucers represented the fear of Communism in the 1950s, now there are other ways of expressing our island nation's fear of the other, of the alien, of the foreign.

So stories about immigrants fall into this story type. But unlike jellyfish or ladybirds or ash clouds, immigrants are human beings like us, which is why it's important that newspapers get it right about their impact. I'm not saying there isn't a debate to be had about the impact of immigration, but if we're to have one, let's have one in which immigrants aren't depicted as invaders or swan-eating savages or people who take all our jobs and go straight to the front of the housing queue. Because that mythology is wrong and panders to prejudice. It might sell a few papers to people who believe those things, but it is wrong, demonstrably wrong, and discredits the whole profession of journalism to see skewed agenda-driven stories like that.

So as ever, it may be the case that readers are just being scared, that they're having their expectations met, that they're telling the newspapers what to think rather than the newspapers telling them what to think, but when you see the same kind of thing, again and again, you have to wonder where one ends and the other begins.

---

[91] The 'Vilecano' front page in the Mirror was a surprising example of this, pointing to a supposedly human face.

Front pages of Daily Express and Daily Star, including headlines MIGRANTS TAKE ALL NEW JOBS (AND THEY GO STRAIGHT TO THE FRONT OF THE HOUSING QUEUE), KEEP OUT – BRITAIN IS FULL UP, ONE IN 5 BRITONS WILL BE ETHNICS, THEY'VE STOLEN ALL OUR JOBS, MUSLIM SCHOOLS BAN OUR CULTURE, BBC PUTS MUSLIMS BEFORE YOU, WHITE MEN TO FACE JOBS BAN, and STRANGERS IN OUR OWN COUNTRY.

Some newspapers, for example, repeatedly tell stories like MIGRANTS TAKE ALL NEW JOBS with the strapline AND THEY GO STRAIGHT TO THE FRONT OF THE HOUSING QUEUE. As you can imagine, those statements fall apart like a wet paper bag under any scrutiny, even though they're seemingly presented as facts, albeit facts on the front page of a newspaper, which perhaps isn't quite as much of a fact as a fact you'll see elsewhere.

If you look at the language used, there's an 'us and them' situation and narrative being set up. BBC PUTS MUSLIMS BEFORE YOU, because YOU are not a Muslim. If you look at a term like 'ethnic', it's basically meaningless because everyone's an 'ethnic' – but there's a deeper meaning in there, a meaning that harks back to ethnic minorities, a meaning that looks back to the days when 'ethnic' was used as a kind of slur. And yes, I know, I know: it's not that easy to get long words and caveats and all of that into a headline, and it could be construed as misleading to judge a newspaper's entire content based on a front-page headline, but the front-page headline is the shop window of the newspaper – it's selling you what's inside. And sometimes the contents are not just representative of these kinds of headline, but even worse.

Now the trouble here is, even if these newspapers are simply meeting the expectations of their readers, they are creating a false perception of what's going on. They are saying things which are demonstrably inaccurate, time after time, so often that it can't be dismissed as simply not having enough room or being an accident. They may well not, in themselves, change people's minds, and I think it would be misleading to say they are; but they add to a conversation in which the same views are being put across again and again.

Because the English Defence League uses articles by the Daily Mail, Daily Express and Daily Star to justify its actions and its campaigns. If you look at the reaction on the Stormfront messageboard, for example, to stories like these from the Express and the Star, you find it's overwhelmingly positive. They're pleased they're being told they're right. They are pleased that they are being rewarded and that finally some people are seeing the truth over immigration. They are rejoicing in the coverage, even though it doesn't stand to scrutiny. They use the trust that people still have for newspapers as a way of saying these trusted sources are agreeing with them. They don't care about that. And maybe that's why we should care.

Getting it wrong

When two teenagers died suddenly on March 17, 2010, there was no doubt in the minds of certain sections of the press as to what had killed them:

MEOW MEOW KILLS 2 TEENS – BAN DRUG NOW (The Sun)

MEOW MEOW KILLS TWO FRIENDS (Metro)

It wasn't just those two papers that decided they could safely conclude the cause of death without waiting for an investigation or an inquest. A trusted police source had said that the deaths were caused by mephedrone, or meow meow, so that was the cause of death – regardless of those troublesomely painstaking toxicology tests, and so on. No, there wasn't time to wait, and there was a deadline approaching, so: *Meow meow kills two teens.*[92]

So if you just get your news from the Sun, you'd be pretty sure that meow meow had killed the pair. Not only that, but there was a lot of concern about this "killer drug", and there was a race to get it banned, which dovetailed in nicely with the Sun's call to ban the drug on March 17.

---

92 The most excellent media blogger Tabloid Watch wrote (http://tabloid-watch.blogspot.com/2011/07/suns-editorials-on-norway.html) on how the Sun had decided, despite very sketchy evidence, that the Norwegian massacre of July 2011 was an 'Al Qaeda' attack, and wrote an editorial stating that the threat of terrorism, "the scourge of the West", meant that there should be no let-up in security ahead of the Olympics, and the Government should press ahead with a change in the law. A few hours later, when the reality became clear, the editorial was altered online.

But on May 28, those toxicology tests finally came back. And they revealed that the two dead men had not, in fact, taken meow meow. This was reported by the BBC and other news sources, but it didn't make the Sun's front page, as the original story had done. The Sun also didn't report on the inquests into the two men's deaths, which were held in January this year. They were reported by some media, more particularly the local press, the Scunthorpe Telegraph. The inquest was told that while the two men had attempted to obtain mephedrone, they had in fact died as a result of drinking alcohol and taking methadone, the heroin substitute, which has a similar name but is a different drug.

Now, I'm not saying that meow meow is a benign drug, and what evidence we do have would suggest that it can pose a risk at high doses, particularly to people who have chronic heart problems. So it's not completely safe or something that people should go around sprinkling on their cornflakes. The Sun may simply have been trying to do society some good by insisting that the drug be banned, even before it had been confirmed that it was responsible for the teenagers' deaths. And they weren't being deliberately misleading – they were acting in good faith on information they received from a trusted source, in this case the police.

But the fact remains that they got it wrong. It was only a front-page story when meow meow was thought to be responsible, not when it was found not to be.

So why did the Sun get the story wrong, and why was it such a big story in the first place? You have to bear in mind this was the front page of the newspaper. That's the shop window for selling a story. On a front-page tabloid splash there isn't room for nuance, or doubt – MEOW

MEOW KILLS TWO TEENS. They're trying to sell the story, and with the story, the newspaper. So let's see why they picked that story. What did the other newspapers report that day?

> *The Independent – SCALE OF YOUTH CRIME SUPPRESSED UNTIL AFTER ELECTION*
> *Telegraph – STUDENT FEES CAP MUST GO, SAYS PATTEN*
> *The Times – NO UNIVERSITY PLACES FOR 50,000 WITH GOOD GRADES*
> *Guardian – QUARTER OF NHS TRUSTS FAIL HYGIENE TESTS*
> *Daily Mail – FATAL BLUNDER OF FOREIGN DOCTOR*
> *Daily Express – ICE COLD GAS 'KILLS' CANCER*
> *Daily Mirror – KATE'S FURY AT SAM'S GIRL PAL (Kate Winslet)*
> *Daily Star – POSH & BECKS WORLD CUP BABY (there was no baby)*

So all the national newspapers went for different stories. That tells us there wasn't a particularly strong story or news event out there which made itself an obvious front-page lead. The Mirror and Star went for celebrity stories; the Independent and Times education stories; the Guardian, Mail and Express health stories. The Telegraph ran the meow meow story as a second lead on its front page, and also linked the teenagers' death with having taken it. So why did the Sun choose that story? And why would readers choose to buy it?

Here are the elements that go together in this story, which, we should remember, is about two human beings' lives being tragically cut short, then exploited to try and flog a few newspapers.

> *DEATH - two people have been killed*
> *TEENAGERS MISBEHAVING / CRIMINAL ACTIVITY - young adults breaking society's moral code and being 'punished'*
> *DRUGS DEATH - two people have died apparently after taking drugs, it's what parents fear most.*
> *LEGAL KILLER - they apparently took a legal drug and died afterwards*
> *PANIC - there's a substance out there, which teenagers are taking, which is lethal*
> *CALL FOR A BAN - newspaper positions itself on 'correct' side of moral argument*
> *UNUSUAL/NEW - more out of the ordinary than e.g. drink driving, heroin death; meow meow hasn't been heard of very much before*

So this story is, at the same time, familiar and unusual. It satisfies readers' expectations while tapping into their fears. Here's a drug we don't know much about, but which is apparently lethal, even though it's completely legal. Some teenagers have been misbehaving and have paid with their lives. It could happen to any family. Parents will be worried. Will your teenage children be going out tonight and taking this drug? Will they come home alive? That's why it hits home. Fear is the key for this type of story. Fear it could happen to you, or someone you know. That's the ghost train.

There are a few reasons why newspapers get science stories wrong. Because they're pressed for time, they can't check things in time; because they report on press releases, rather than analysing the reports for themselves; because even if they had the time and the reports, the journalists wouldn't always have the range of skills to go through these reports scientifically; that readers are too stupid to understand, and must have everything oversimplified for them, and so on. Some commentators say that because journalists largely come from a humanities background rather than a science background, they lack the skill set to cover science stories properly. And there may well be something in that.

But there is also another explanation. The other explanation is that they simply don't care whether what they're saying is true or not – they're there to sell you a type of truth, rather than tell you the whole truth, to meet your expectations rather than to confound you. An "X gives you cancer" story is just a type of story. It's a narrative that works and which readers expect and understand. Avoid all complexity. It is one or the other. Then it's a story. Remove all nuance, all caveats, all doubt. X gives you cancer. X prevents cancer. There it is.

Not only that, but the newspaper may well be set up to present the kinds of narratives it believes its readers want to see – the kind of things they expect and demand. It confirms what people already think; people seek out those opinions which most closely match their own prejudices and sometimes fears, as I've said. So the individual reporter is a small part of that. They may well write a story full of caveats and nuances, all of which are taken out, because the simplified story is a better narrative, or a more understandable one for the target readership.

A reporter may be instructed to write a story in a certain kind of way, or find a particular angle, whether it's there or not, because that's what is expected, and that's what the readers want. As a part of a corporate culture of compliance, they will do what they are told. There's also the idea of anticipatory compliance, where people learn what is expected of them and behave accordingly.

So there are many reasons why newspapers get it wrong. They may not want to get it right in the first place. They might not care about whether it's right or not. They may simply want to use the bare facts to tell the story they want to tell, rather than the story that actually was there. They may not have the whole picture. They may be lazy. The reporters may simply be told that's what the readers want. And of course it may be the case that readers will only buy what they want to see. In which case it's our fault, as punters, in a way.

And there's another very important point to make about newspapers getting it wrong. Not all newspapers get it wrong. Even the newspapers that do get things wrong don't get them wrong all the time. And most journalists are hardworking, underpaid, overworked, undervalued people. The vast majority of things you read in a newspaper will be entirely accurate. But all that said, things do go wrong. And when they do, they taint the whole profession.

The future

So what we've looked at so far are the reasons why newspapers are in a decline of trust, and there are many others. One reason why newspapers are starting to fall apart is that they represent a very one-way flow of information. There is a story, you're told what the story is, you read the story, and that's that. You can write a letter to the newspaper if you think they've got it wrong, but that can easily be ignored or swept under the carpet. But people are getting more and more used to interactive media. My 92-year-old next-door neighbour, who just reads the Sun and doesn't get his news from anywhere else, is becoming the exception rather than the rule. That's not to say he doesn't just think it's all a load of rubbish anyway, even though he reads it, or that he buys the Sun just for the sport, or for page 3, or whatever. It's easy to imagine that readers are just passive consumers, because of the one-way flow of information, and simply believe what they're told, but I think it's a bit more complicated than that. However, newspapers do represent a one-way flow of information to readers and consumers, and consumers are demanding more and more interactivity in media nowadays.

But there's another decline, too, a decline of circulation and a decline of revenue, which isn't entirely connected to a decline of trust, but isn't a million miles away from it, either. Many national newspapers have been running at a considerable loss for years, and that process is only accelerating as advertisers find other ways to push their products than putting them in newspapers with falling sales. Digital revenues aren't enough, either; the only websites that manage to make money online are those which have content heavy with celebrity stories and paparazzi pictures.

The Daily Mail gets huge online traffic, mostly for its celebrity stories, of which there are dozens every day, often involving celebrities that aren't even familiar to British readers. That's how you monetise the digital platform, not with groundbreaking news and investigations. That's a sadness for those of us who passionately believe in investigative journalism, but once again, just as with newspapers, it's all about giving the people what they want. If they want pictures of Kim Kardashian in a bikini or Katy Perry walking along the street, that's what they are going to get. It may be depressing, but that's what happens when you tie in journalism with revenue. You can't make people like things they don't like.

Newspaper operations are shrinking. Staff have been cut down the years, so now there are fewer staff attempting to produce more pages, more editions, more online stuff, more everything. National newspapers may survive by cross media promotion, you may get the Times bundled in with your Sky TV subscription, for example, if News Corporation succeeds in its bid for BSkyB, and there's cross ownership with Richard Desmond at Channel 5, with the Express, the Star and OK! Magazine, we've already seen that with OK! TV starting up. That's how they're looking to the future – newspapers as part of the product, not the whole product. Local newspapers, on the other hand, remain extremely profitable, though only because thousands of jobs are being shed all the time. They're clinging on to unrealistic profit margins by slashing jobs, eventually something has got to give, and now readers have noticed and circulations are declining by double digits. Local papers don't have to disappear, but they are disappearing too.

So if newspapers are to disappear, what or who will replace them? And what does that mean for trusted news sources? Well, as we've seen, not all news sources can be considered trustworthy in the first place. Some newspapers distort the truth because it's simpler; some tell you a version of the truth that they think you'd prefer;

some simply make it up. Consumers are becoming more and more used to mistrusting newspapers – mistrusting all sources, treating all the imposters just the same. Which is a healthy and positive thing, I think.

The good thing for us as consumers is that there's more choice than ever – more choice over what to read, where to get our information and where to find our news. And we can get it wherever and whenever we want. Look at the way that social media combined with traditional media are having such an impact on the democracy campaigns in the middle east, for example, and it seems encouraging. Traditional journalists are brave to put their heads above the parapet, and face abuse and violence.

People are aware of this, they have the tools to make their own news now. And I think there's plenty to be excited about with that. It's easy for journalists to sneer at bloggers and users of social media as the uninformed, but the power balance is shifting, the tide is coming in. Writing isn't actually that hard, most people are discovering, and they want to get their voices out there. The better it is, the more people will see it; people read you because they want to read you, not out of any brand loyalty or dailiness. That's the excitement. It makes for a more engaged consumer of news and information and comment, someone who says, I am the one who will decide what I read and when. I don't want horoscopes chucked in with investigative journalism. I don't want to read about celebrity gossip. Or I do. I don't want rugby league reports alongside football. Or I do.

Life after newspapers is exciting. As a journalist, I hope there's still a place for investigative journalism, really good writing and reportage. But I don't think it matters what I hope. We won't decide that. The readers will decide. Instead of giving them what we think they want, they will decide what they want to read, and we'll know about it. The reason why people fell out of love with newspapers was because they try to provide a version of the truth acceptable to what they think their readers want to see, rather than what's there. In an age where people can source original documents and data in seconds, that was always going to fall apart and reduce the credibility of the brands involved in doing that. So the battle for the few remaining readers sees these positions even more entrenched. Meanwhile, the rest of us are getting our news elsewhere.

There's also another thing to say about life after newspapers. The email inviting me here this evening came on the day I was told I was going to be made redundant from the newspaper I work for at the moment. And seeing as there are no jobs to be had around here, not anywhere I'd work anyway, that means I'm no longer working in newspapers myself. I have my own life after newspapers, and blogging is all I have. Which isn't terrible – as one someone said to me, you haven't ceased to be a journalist, you've just become more freelance than before. I like that way of looking at things. And I like being able to write in a way that isn't restricted by the needs of an employer, to say what I like. Life after newspapers for me could be a very good thing. It has to be. I hope it will be for all of us.

Not a journalist any more

As I write this, I'm hurtling towards redundancy – towards a place where I don't know where the money is going to come from, or what I'm going to do. That is a frightening and a liberating thing. While I enjoy the structure of work, and having a workplace, I also like the fact that sometimes it's nice not to have to commute, to trundle along the M4 and nearly fall asleep at the wheel, to get your employment from something other than turning up in the same place every day. That's what I tell myself, anyway, but I really want to have a job. Just a little job. That can't be so hard, can it?

Well, it turns out it can. I sent my CV off to an employment agency the other week, and they offered me a job at an abattoir. That kind of took the wind out of my sails a bit. There really isn't a great deal around that looks like nourishing employment, and I don't really fancy the idea of chopping up chickens for a living, so I might be 'a little bit more freelance than I'd anticipated', by which I mean unemployed.

It's not just me, of course, who's been laid off. Jobs are falling apart in all sectors, in all places, but local newspapers and the people who work there are suffering more than most. I could go into the hows and whys, and launch some kind of limp-wristed shaking fist at the owners who want nothing but profit, and have decided to run down the products in order to keep profit levels artificially high, but what would that achieve? The industry is in decline, and while there are hundreds of people graduating with media-type degrees, like me, there simply aren't the jobs there for them, or me.

I think things are changing. Journalists aren't going to be as tied to profit-making newspapers as much as they once were. I think things like sub-editors are becoming something of a luxury. That's a shame for a couple of reasons: firstly, because that's what I chose to specialise in, and secondly, because I think even the best writers need a good editor, or another pair of eyes over their stuff. Sometimes we all need to be told that the thing we've slaved over isn't as good as we thought it was; sometimes we all need our copy chucked back at us and told to re-write. But that happens less and less. What you're left with is people like me. Ghastly.

And I think people are taking it into their own hands to publish what they want – either through blogging, or through self-publishing books like this. You don't need someone else's permissions to be able to say what you want to say, because the tools are available to everyone nowadays. And I think that's a positive thing. I wish that in a way there would be a place for quality investigative journalism, and everything that brings with it, but I have no idea whether that really will stay around or not. I'll look back at this in a few years' time, or maybe someone will find this book in a massive landfill pile in the middle of nowhere, and look at it like I look at JC Cannell's writing – a relic from another age, where everything was very different.

Which means I'm not a journalist any more. When I was

younger, it was all I wanted to be, and all that I wanted to do. I just wanted to write, and write, and never stop, and somehow everything would fall together, and it would all be OK. But it didn't work out that way. Here, at the age of 36, I'm looking at a future in which I might not be a journalist at all, if I can find any kind of job, and it's hard to see a way back into the industry I joined back in 1999, when I was much younger, and much more naïve, and much more immature.

If not a journalist, what can I be? Well, I know people who've moved on into all kinds of other fields, and they've done perfectly well. They've used the skills that journalism has taught them – and it does teach you skills – to good effect in other careers and other professions. I suppose journalism teaches you to be sceptical about what other people tell you; it teaches you to try and be thorough about what you're presenting (or at least what I would regard as good journalism does).

It taught me that you can get a glimpse of those things you dream about – in my case, that was being a football reporter for the local paper, smelling the half-time pies burning away while watching a game under floodlights, from massive stadiums to tiny little fleapits next to the allotments. And it's given me the opportunity to write in a way that I never thought I could, and spread that around to a wide audience. I've been very lucky. My career, while a mediocre failure by most standards, has provided me with an awful lot of pleasure. More than anything I just remember the people – the fellow journalists who have made me roar with laughter, who have become good friends, who have been there for me in spirit despite all of the depression and all of the problems I've written about here. That, for me, is what I am going to miss most.

But I am not a journalist any more. Maybe a writer, but not a journalist. I don't really belong to a newspaper, or a publication, so I am just a writer, looking for somewhere to write. In the absence of a benefactor, I'll write wherever and whenever I can. Blogging has taught me that you can just write, and write, and write, and write for yourself – and it provides a huge amount of satisfaction. Perhaps not the same satisfaction as seeing your words as inky splodges on a page, but I'll take it.

All I can do is be grateful for the career that I have had, and look forward to whatever it is that's next. Thanks for reading, thanks for replying, thanks for commenting, thanks for being patient, thanks for putting up with me. And goodbye journalism, I'll miss you.

Hastily-cobbled-together chapter on phonehacking

Kaboom. Kaboom after kaboom after kaboom. It seemed during the crazy days of summer in 2011 that the kabooms would never stop; that it would be impossible to stop the tide. But now, a couple of weeks after the phonehacking row saw the News of the World consigned to the dustbin, I suppose it's possible to take a look back and see what kind of landscape is left by it all.

Phonehacking took time to take off with the public. It seemed it was one of those things that was a minor trifle to be pored over by Guardian readers or people inside the London media bubble, but no more than that; no matter what kind of revelation the likes of Nick Davies could drag up about the press, the story just didn't have legs. People weren't interested, beyond the kind of people who had an interest in being interested; even the connection between Andy Coulson and David Cameron didn't make it any more intriguing for common morons on the street like you and me. But it was the angle that the phone of dead schoolgirl Milly Dowler may have been hacked – and messages possibly deleted, giving false hope to her family – that really changed everything, from a story of limited interest into a seriously big deal. It was when I saw people discussing it on This Morning that I knew it had become a story that went beyond something that a few lefties would pontificate about on Twitter and achieve nothing by doing so. Punters, it seems, can tolerate the phones of celebrities being hacked, and at a push they don't mind politicians being pried upon – but when it comes to someone like a missing teenager, who was later found to have been murdered, that's a different matter altogether. This was, all of a sudden, the only story in town. Those who had sat back and imagined it was all going to go away were going to get a nasty shock. It wasn't going to go away – and the reason it wasn't was because it had become a 'story'.

It's ironic that it would be quality investigative journalism that would cause the demise of the News of the World. But they themselves had created a culture in which accusation became supposition which then became fact; so many times had they set up a line of dots and asked readers to join them, and so many times had they 'passed their dossier to police' and invited readers to draw their own conclusions that you couldn't help not feeling sorry for them. Their readers, then, were only doing what they had been taught to do by the News of the World itself – they could see the circumstantial evidence, and they drew their own conclusions; they weren't going to wait for the outcome of an internal investigation to decide whether or not there was culpability. When punters saw the News of the Screws being linked to the hacking of a dead child's phone, they didn't like what they saw.

By targeting advertisers and explaining the toxification of the environment for brands that the News of the World had become through the scandal, campaigners managed the seemingly unthinkable – to haul down the paper itself. It probably wasn't the intention of many campaigners, and even among those for whom it was, it was very much a dream; but there it was. The News of the World had become a dirty, stinking maggot-ridden albatross; a profit-making paper had become something that needed to be jettisoned as soon as possible. Revisionists might look back on this decision and see it as a way of hastening the demise of something that was going to die anyway, of speeding up the merger between the weekly and Sunday operations, and I think there may be some truth in that; but one thing is for certain – this wasn't the way that anyone involved had expected or wanted the News of the World to go out of business, reviled and untouchable.

The final NOTW was defiant, portraying itself as very much on the side of the angels, and very much the victim in all of this – and it sold by the bucketload. People eagerly snapped up a 'souvenir' edition, along with millions of others, hoping that one day it might fetch more than the cover price on Ebay. But no-one was advertising in it, and the scandal had tainted the brand, so much so that other brands didn't want to be associated with it. This wasn't a shadowy cabal of leftist troublemakers sabotaging a much-loved British institution; nor was this the liberal elite attempting to chip away at the Murdoch empire they were so jealous of; the simple truth was that the allegations of hacking were too damaging, and there was worse to come as the days went by.

This wasn't much comfort for the hardworking hacks who'd been left on the scrapheap by the decision to close the Screws. I know it's easy to say that people shouldn't have worked for the paper in the first place, but I do feel sorry for anyone who loses their job in the way they did. It's not easy to find another one, especially in the media, at the moment, as I am discovering. And besides, a lot of the journalists who were kicked out weren't responsible for the kind of trashy stuff that was at the heart of the phonehacking and other allegations – they were just trying to earn a living. I can't bring myself to find any joy in the loss of their jobs, not at all. When the Sport and Sunday Sport closed (though the Sunday version is back up and running, at the time of writing) I didn't feel much sympathy at all: those publications are pure crap, written for masturbation and seriously tawdry rubbish; the NOTW, whatever you think of it, had its good aspects – I know I've bought it in the past for its sports coverage, when I want to read something about my team rather than Manchester United.

But that was that. The Screws was put in the dustbin, and it was hoped that might bring a seemly transition towards a seven-day Sun, or whatever project would fill the void left behind by the biggest-selling newspaper in the country having been wound up in a week. In the meantime, there was a scramble for readers. But the same questions remained. Who knew what? Who was in charge? Did the people in charge know anything, or nothing? What evidence was there still to be found? What skeletons were lurking in the News of the World closet? And what would happen to the News Corporation bid for BSkyB?

It remains to be seen what the final fallout of all this will be, but I think one of the interesting aspects has been the gulf between perception and reality in all of this. Newspapers have always, I think, felt that their readers would understand what was going on in their name, or wouldn't be interested enough in trifling matters of media ethics enough to care about how their stories arrived. But that has changed now. The perception was always that readers didn't really care how the stories got into the newspaper on the breakfast table, as long as they were good tales; the reality is probably not quite that at all. Readers can get their news from a dozen other places, and they need a good reason to get a paper. If that paper is seen to be acting unscrupulously, that is a deterrent to loyalty. Why stay loyal to someone who's going to do that, or who's so inept that they didn't know it was going on? What can we believe, when so many people are looking the other way, all the time?

But newspaper readers are not stupid, nor are they a giant blob of cookie-cutter folk who all go out like a pack of chimps and buy the same paper week after week, regardless of what's inside. Tabloid readers are readers, after all; they're getting their news written down rather than just looking at some pretty pictures on the tellybox – although sometimes, sure, people are just looking at the pretty pictures. Some folk expected the NOTW readers to go skipping off to the newsagents despite all the scandal and unthinkingly buy the paper as usual. But that didn't happen: those readers could hear about the story from elsewhere – it was even reported in the Sun, not through choice but through stone-cold necessity – and make their choices accordingly. Sure, the 'collector's edition' sold out – the 168-year-old newspaper finished on a high. But it wouldn't have been that way, had it not been the final ever copy.

A lot of perceptions have shifted. The Rupert Murdoch empire was previously seen to be an huge monolith, a fortress, an impenetrable and indefatigable thing that would last forever. Murdoch always got it right, and didn't make mistakes, whatever you thought of him. That was the old certainty, at least; but now, that doesn't seem to be the case, at all. Murdoch seems as vulnerable and as liable to make mistakes as anyone else. The aura, for want of a better word, has been tarnished, even if it hasn't disappeared completely. But it's strange how someone can look invincible one moment, and decidedly shaky the next. Murdoch will probably survive, but not unscathed.

I wonder what else will happen with relation to press regulation and press freedom. I don't think there's a huge public appetite, despite all this, to dismantle the Press Complaints Commission and create a new regulatory body; and we should of course be wary of allowing any kind of restriction on press freedom to be brought in by using the phonehacking scandals as a convenient jemmy with which to break the door open. Then again, it may be another one of those things where the lofty arguments about freedom and newspapers being able to hold the Government to account don't really stack up against the reality of newspapers wanting to intrude on famous people's private lives and tell you who's been having sex with whom. We are always told that it's what the punters want, that we get the press we deserve, and so on – and maybe that is true. But that doesn't mean that there isn't a demand for the murkier side of Fleet Street to just be able to get away with whatever they want, in the unlikely event that one day they might accidentally unearth something of democratic value.

The trouble is, newspapers don't always do what they say they do. They don't always hold the powerful to account; sometimes they're cosying up with the powerful in order to get what they want. They tell you how to vote, but they don't tell you the real reasons why; they tell you it's for your own good, but more often than not you end up wondering if it's really in their interests to tell you to put your X in a particular box. We all know this, and this is no great revelation; we've been taking what they say with a pinch of salt since year dot. Yes, in theory newspapers and the printed media are a great way of safeguarding democracy, but in reality, that's not always the case. On the other hand, the exposure of the phonehacking scandal couldn't have been done without real investigative journalism, followed up by a lot of digging by the quality press – not just the Guardian, but others too.

I think there is a sense, as I'm writing this, that there is a feeling that something needs to be done, and that something might involve some kind of regulation other than the self-regulation of the Press Complaints Commission; but whether this will be lost in the length of time it takes for a report to come out about this whole business, or an inquiry to find fault or otherwise, remains to be seen. We just don't know what else will come to light, or what the public appetite for change will be at a point in the future.

Where does all this leave us, then? I think the scandals have eroded credibility in journalism in general – despite the fact that good journalists uncovered the whole mess, and despite the fact that a lot of hardworking journalists got sent down to the Jobcentre through no fault of their own. It matters because this story went beyond the media bubble, and newspapers were subjected to scrutiny as never before. When people looked under the rock, they didn't like what they saw squirming and wriggling underneath. What they saw and heard were people in charge trying to say that everything was all right, when that didn't add up with the evidence they were reading about and hearing about from elsewhere. People lost what little trust they had left. Bad journalism tarnishes the whole profession. It's what I've been saying for years, rabbiting on mostly to myself on my silly little blog, but there it is:

the actions of the minority do taint the image of the majority. On the whole, I think journalists are a decent bunch – I used to be one, after all, and many of my best friends are still hacking away, god love them. It's not the scandal that has made journalism look bad; it's the bad journalists.

But the damage has been done, and it needs repairing. After Diana's death, papers made lofty claims that they wouldn't touch long-lens paparazzi photographs, but after a suitable amount of time had passed, the grainy pap photos began finding their way onto the pages and onto the websites, just as they had done before. Will this all go quietly away, only to resurface at a future date? Or have we really had enough of sharp practices?

As I said in the previous chapter, newspapers are dying – it's not the end for them quite yet, but this is another milestone along the way to their eventual demise, whenever that might be. Time was when you could just shrug your shoulders and say that the punters would be back, but the world is a different place now. If you don't like where you're getting your news from, you can select another channel very rapidly, and that's the end of that. Newspapers need to be seen to be ethical and responsible, and to match the aspirations of their readers. The phonehacking scandal saw perceptions shift. Whether they have shifted for good, we don't know yet; but things probably won't be the same again.

Thanks

For reading this. Thanks for reading the blog in the first place, if you did. Thanks for putting up with me when I was being a pain, or being annoying or vexatious or rambled about stuff you didn't care about. Thanks for all of that, and I really appreciate it. Thanks to all the bloggers who have helped with advice and support and links and everything down the years – there are far too many to name but you know who you are, and all the help (and criticism) you gave was really important for me. Thanks to the people I love most, for understanding that I do love writing, and that occasionally it's going to be something that takes up a lot of time. All the patience and kindness, love and support has meant the world to me. And thanks to everyone who wrote in, left a comment, sent me a link, sent me an email, gave a donation, or did anything. This is maybe the end of one era but the beginning of another. I hope to write more – not like this, but new stuff, moving in new directions.

So, here goes.

Printed in Great Britain
by Amazon.co.uk, Ltd.,
Marston Gate.